FAITH UNDER FIRE
A MEMOIR

SCOTT HAYES

Copyright © 2025 by Scott Hayes

All rights reserved.

No portion of this book may be reproduced in any form without written permission from the publisher or author, except as permitted by U.S. copyright law.

Contents

Dedication ... 1

The Rebbe ... 3

Introduction ... 5

Prologue ... 9

1. Chapter 1: ... 13
   Roots in Brookline — Contradictions of Childhood

2. Chapter 2 ... 19
   Faith at the Crossroads — Identity in Question

3. Chapter 3: ... 25
   Marching Into Uniform — Duty Over Self

4. Chapter 4: ... 33
   Shadows Over Bosnia — Witness to Division

5. Chapter 5: ... 47
   Kosovo's Dividing Lines — Boundaries of Blood

6. Chapter 6: ... 57
   Baptized by War — Faith in Fire

7. Chapter 7: ... 73
   Return to Iraq — Scars Reopened

8. Chapter 8: 81
A Zionist Awakens — Convictions Forged

9. Chapter 9: 95
The Breaking Point — Shattered but Unbowed

10. Chapter 10: 107
Stars and Stripes — Star of David

11. Chapter 11: 117
Brotherhood in Black Hats — Embraced in Faith

12. Chapter 12: 129
The Gathering Storm — Darkness Approaches

13. Chapter 13: 146
September 12, 2024 — Flashpoint

14. Chapter 14: 159
Terror in Newton — Blood on the Pavement

15. Chapter 15: 170
Chains of Injustice — The Arraignment

16. Chapter 16: 177
Shackled at Home — Prison Without Bars

17. Chapter 17: 190
Between Rockets and Roots — Israel Under Fire

18. Chapter 18: 215
Witch Hunt — Marian Ryan's Revenge

19. Chapter 19: 225
Still Standing — Faith Prevails

Epilogue 229

Acknowledgements	231
About the author	233

For my mother and my daughter—the two pillars of my life.
And for the Jewish people, whose strength and resilience inspire me always to stand with you.

The Rebbe

"In a time of increasing darkness, we must respond with an increasing of light." – The Lubavitcher Rebbe

Introduction

This is my story.

It is the story of how an ordinary man—raised in a small Massachusetts town, shaped by family, faith, and service—found himself caught in the crosshairs of a conflict much larger than himself. It is the story of how I went from being a private citizen, a father, a worker like anyone else, to becoming a public figure thrust into the spotlight—not by choice, not by ambition, but by tragedy, violence, and conviction.

I never set out to write these words. For years, I lived a quiet life. I believed in hard work, in taking care of my family, in living by principles instilled in me long ago. I never chased the kind of attention that now surrounds me. But the events of September 12, 2024, and everything that spiraled out from them, made silence impossible. To stay silent would have meant surrender—to hate, to fear, and to those who would rather see people like me erased. And that, I could not allow.

At the heart of it all is my unwavering support for Israel and the Jewish people. That support is not casual or abstract; it is woven into my identity as deeply as any thread of faith or patriotism. Over the years, I have come to see Israel not just as a nation in the Middle East, but as an idea: a beacon of survival, resilience, and renewal against impossible odds. The Jewish people's story, with its cycles of exile and return, of persecution and persistence, resonated with me in ways I could not ignore.

Those beliefs, which I hold proudly and without apology, ultimately cost me more than I ever could have imagined. They cost me peace. They cost me safety. They cost me privacy. And on one harrowing afternoon, they nearly cost me my life. What happened to me was not an accident. It was not a misunderstanding. It was not the result of miscommunication or tempers flaring. It was the deliberate act of a radicalized individual—an act of domestic terrorism—committed for no other reason than the fact that I stood with Israel and the Jewish people.

I never wanted fame. I never wanted cameras in my face, or my name dragged across the internet, or to be dissected in courtrooms and newsrooms. What I wanted was simple: to stand shoulder to shoulder with friends and neighbors, Jews and non-Jews alike, in defense of truth, dignity, and democracy. I wanted to raise my voice against antisemitism, against lies about Israel, against the normalization of hatred. I wanted to live in alignment with what I knew to be right.

But standing for something in today's world is never simple. In doing so, I found myself marked. I found myself the target not only of an attacker's fist, but of an entire system ready to twist reality, to smear me, and to turn the victim into the accused.

And yet, in the darkness, I found light. I found strength I did not know I had. I found solidarity in the Jewish community, in strangers who became brothers and sisters, in allies who refused to let me stand alone. Faith carried me. Purpose sustained me. And above all, the community gave me reason to endure.

This book would not exist without the unshakable love and support I received during the most painful and uncertain chapter of my life. Jewish communities across Massachusetts—and beyond—opened their arms when others turned away. They prayed for me when I was confined. They wrote letters, made calls, and showed up in courtrooms. Their encouragement was not just comforting—it was life-saving. When the system tried to crush me, it was the people who lifted me back to my feet. This is as much their story as it is mine.

I write these pages for several reasons. First, to tell the truth of what happened. My name and reputation were dragged through the mud, twisted into headlines that bore little resemblance to reality. This is my chance to reclaim my voice, to put the record straight.

But beyond that, I write to warn. To warn others that silence in the face of hate is never an option. Antisemitism is not an abstract concept—it is a living, breathing hatred that mutates, adapts, and strikes wherever it finds weakness. It is not someone else's problem, nor is it confined to the pages of history books. It is here, now, on our streets, in our schools, in our politics. What happened to me was not isolated—it was part of a broader pattern, one that should alarm every American who cares about freedom and justice.

I also write to inspire. Not because I see myself as a hero—I do not—but because I know firsthand how quickly despair can take root when the world turns upside down. I know what it feels like to sit in a cell, accused of crimes you did not commit, wondering if your life is over. I know the exhaustion of fighting a battle you never asked for. And I also know the power of refusing to give up. If my story can give strength to even one person facing their own struggle—whether against hatred, injustice, or personal hardship—then this book will have served its purpose.

Finally, I write to honor. To honor those who stood by me, to honor those who continue to stand for Israel and the Jewish people, to honor the values that guided me even when the cost was unbearable. This book is an offering of gratitude, a record of survival, and a call to action.

This is my story and now, it is yours too.

Prologue

September 12, 2024 began like any other ordinary workday.

The sun rose gently over Massachusetts, casting the same muted light it had on countless mornings before. I woke early, as I always did, and prepared for another day at work. My job was not glamorous, but it was steady: I worked as a contractor for National Grid, handling inspection and detection tasks. The work required attention to detail, patience, and consistency. It was the kind of job that kept the lights on—literally—for thousands of homes and businesses. It was important, though hardly the sort of work anyone outside the company would notice.

That morning unfolded without incident. I put on my uniform, grabbed my gear, and headed out. The tasks blurred together, routine and familiar. Check equipment. Record data. Move to the next site. Eat lunch on the go. Nothing stood out, nothing hinted at what was to come. It was, in every way, an ordinary Thursday.

But ordinary days have a way of breaking without warning.

When my shift ended, I changed out of work mode and into another role I had come to embrace in recent years: advocate, supporter, ally. I headed to Newton, Massachusetts, where a small group of us had organized a peaceful demonstration of solidarity with Israel and the Jewish people. The chosen site was the intersection of Harvard and Washington Streets—a crossroads of traffic and visibility, a place where thousands of commuters flowed daily. We wanted our presence to be unmistakable: a reminder to everyone driving past that Israel was not alone, and neither were the Jews of Massachusetts.

The weather could not have been better. The late-summer sun hung warm but not oppressive, casting golden light on our flags and signs. A light breeze carried the sound of passing cars and occasional honks of support. The mood was hopeful, optimistic, proud. We were not a massive crowd, but we were united. We exercised our constitutional right to gather, to speak, to stand visibly against antisemitism and in support of Israel's right to exist.

And then, in an instant, everything changed.

The peace shattered like glass under a hammer.

I remember the shift in the air—the sudden tension, the sense of something bearing down. I remember seeing the attacker, moving with purpose, eyes filled with rage. I remember the blows, sharp and unrelenting, the world tilting as violence erupted out of nowhere. Pain exploded, disorientation followed. In those moments, I was no longer a protester, no longer a worker, no longer just a man standing with a flag. I was a target.

The attack was brutal, calculated, and deeply personal. It was not about me as an individual—it was about what I represented. It was about silencing voices of support for Israel, about instilling fear. It was a hate crime in its purest form, stripped of pretense. And it worked, at least for a moment: I was bloodied, shaken, reeling.

But the story did not end with that attack. In many ways, it began there.

Because what followed was not only the physical toll of violence, but the far heavier weight of betrayal. In the hours and days that followed, I discovered that the system I trusted—the police, the courts, the institutions sworn to protect victims—had turned its back on me. Instead of being treated as the survivor of a hate crime, I was treated as a criminal. I was handcuffed, booked, and smeared. My name became a headline, twisted into something unrecognizable.

That day did not just leave scars on my body—it tore open the illusion that truth and justice are guaranteed. It revealed the fragility of the protections so many of us take for granted.

What follows in this book is not just an account of that day, though it is the beating heart of the narrative. It is the story of everything that led to that moment, and everything that came after. It is a story of conviction, of betrayal, of resilience. It is a story of the cost of standing for what is right in a time when right and wrong are blurred by politics, hatred, and cowardice.

And it all began on one seemingly normal day.

Chapter 1:

Roots in Brookline — Contradictions of Childhood

Brookline, Massachusetts was not just where I grew up—it was where the building blocks of my identity were laid, one block at a time, in ways that would only become clear decades later.

In the late 1970s and 1980s, Brookline was a patchwork town: part city, part suburb, a place where trolley lines and brownstones sat just steps away from leafy side streets and tidy triple-deckers. It was a place where history clung to the bricks, where Fenway's roar drifted through the summer air, and where families—Irish, Jewish, Russian, Italian, all thrown together—learned to coexist in a uniquely New England rhythm.

My family was Irish Catholic, through and through. Faith and tradition weren't optional—they were assumed, part of the air we breathed. Sundays were for Mass, holidays were for church and extended family, and life was measured in sacraments: baptism, first communion, confirmation. The Catholic Church wasn't just where

we prayed—it was the spine of our community, the institution that gave shape to everything else.

Priests weren't just spiritual guides; they were men of authority, whose presence commanded respect whether they were in the pulpit or strolling down Harvard Street in their collars. When a priest walked into a room, conversations quieted. When he spoke, you listened. Nuns weren't just teachers in the classroom; they were disciplinarians, guardians of morality, and keepers of a strict kind of order. Their lessons weren't just academic—they drilled into us notions of obedience, sacrifice, and humility. The mixture of compassion and fear they wielded was deliberate, and for a long time, it worked.

As a boy, I didn't question any of it. The rhythms of Catholic life felt as natural as breathing. You didn't ask why—you just went along because that's what everyone did. The bells of St. Mary's tolled, and families streamed in. Incense hung in the air, mingling with the smell of wet wool coats in winter. You stood, you sat, you knelt, you repeated the responses without really thinking.

But Brookline wasn't just about pews and sacraments. It was also about the streets, the playgrounds, and the small adventures that made up childhood. Summer evenings meant pickup games of street hockey, the sound of sticks clattering against asphalt, and kids yelling "Car!" before dragging the nets to the curb. We played flashlight tag until our parents called us in, sprinting through dark yards with the thrill of being caught just a step away. GI Joes battled in the dirt behind porches and under hedges, epic wars fought between action figures while real-world tensions played out in miniature.

And then there was Eddie the Ice Cream King. Everyone in the neighborhood knew his truck by sound before sight—the jingle of his music echoing off the triple-deckers, sending kids scrambling for loose change. We'd chase his truck down the street, sweaty and breathless, waving quarters in our hands like trophies. Eddie was part businessman, part magician, doling out rocket pops and soft serve cones as if they were treasures. For a few minutes, on those summer nights, everything else faded—the Church, the whispers, even the divorce back home. Childhood was distilled into the taste of melting ice cream on a hot night and the laughter of friends.

But beneath that innocence, my family life was shifting. My parents divorced when I was still young, and that fracture cut through the neat order of sacraments and Sunday Mass. My siblings and I stayed in Brookline with my father, who was not especially devout. That meant that much of the pressure to keep us tied to the rituals came from extended family and from the larger community itself. Divorce in those years still carried a stigma, especially in Irish Catholic circles. It was spoken about in whispers, a quiet mark against a family. For me, it was the first sign that the Church's vision of family didn't always match reality.

Brookline itself was a place of contrasts, and I absorbed those lessons early. Though diverse, the town was not immune to the quiet divisions that ran beneath the surface. Irish kids mostly stuck with Irish kids, Jewish kids with Jewish kids. It wasn't outright hostility, at least not in my neighborhood, but there were invisible lines you could feel. Jokes were made. Stereotypes lingered. Antisemitism wasn't shouted from rooftops anymore the way it might have been in the 1940s or '50s, but it hadn't disappeared either. You could hear it in whispers, in the way adults spoke when they thought children weren't listening.

And I listened. I always listened. I heard uncles make cracks about money at family gatherings. I heard kids repeat things they'd overheard at home, words that made me uncomfortable even if I didn't yet know how to challenge them. Something in me resisted those judgments. Maybe it was because I had Jewish classmates and neighbors, faces I couldn't reconcile with the stereotypes. Maybe it was because I saw something in their eyes—a seriousness, a weight—that made me respect them instinctively.

At Sunday school, I was taught that Jews had rejected Christ, that they were still waiting for a Messiah who had already come. It was presented not as prejudice, but as doctrine, a fact you weren't supposed to question. But the more time I spent around Jewish neighbors, the more narrow that teaching felt. These people weren't "lost" or "stubborn"—they were resilient. They weren't rejecting anything; they were carrying forward something ancient and precious. I began to sense that their strength didn't come from defiance, but from survival.

Brookline made that survival visible. Synagogues dotted the streets. Hebrew letters marked store windows. On Fridays, Jewish families walked to shul in their best clothes, their pace unhurried but purposeful. Through the windows of their homes I saw the glow of Shabbat candles, heard the sound of Hebrew prayers, and sometimes caught laughter that carried down the block. In contrast, my Sundays were marked by incense, wooden pews, and the steady voice of a priest from the pulpit. The two worlds weren't far apart—sometimes separated by only a block or two—but they carried different weights.

By my teenage years, I had developed something like dual loyalty—not in a political sense, but in a personal one. I was still Catholic, still doing my best to walk the path laid out by my family and Saint Marys. But part of me was also drawn toward the Jewish story, the Jewish struggle, the Jewish survival. I didn't have the words for it then, but I knew instinctively: their fight was my fight.

And then came the turning point. By the time I reached eighth grade, the Boston Catholic Church sex abuse scandal was no longer a whisper—it was a tidal wave. The headlines were everywhere. Priests I had once looked up to were suddenly spoken about in shameful tones. Trust, once absolute, collapsed almost overnight. I remember walking past the church one afternoon, staring at the front door, and feeling something I had never felt before: suspicion. Was this priest one of "them"? Were the adults in my parish covering something up? The certainty I had once carried—the idea that the Church was beyond reproach—crumbled.

I stopped going to Mass altogether. At first it was excuses, then outright refusal. It wasn't rebellion for the sake of rebellion. It was disillusionment. The very institution that had been the spine of our family and community now felt hollow,

corrupted, unsafe. If the priests couldn't be trusted, if the leaders of the Church had betrayed the people in their care, then the rituals meant nothing.

Leaving the Church left a hole. But it also opened up space. Into that space came something else—the recognition that the Jewish community around me, the one I had quietly admired for years, had something enduring that I was no longer finding in Catholicism. They had faith, yes, but they also had memory, resilience, solidarity. They weren't untouched by scandal or hardship, but they carried their history openly, without shame, and transformed it into strength.

Brookline gave me more than just exposure to Judaism. It gave me a deep respect for the community itself. Whether it was my parish rallying around a sick family, or Jewish neighbors raising funds for a new synagogue roof, or even just kids sticking up for each other on the basketball court, I saw firsthand that survival required solidarity. Nobody made it alone. Everyone leaned on someone.

That lesson became the backbone of my life. In war zones, in rallies, in courtrooms, I would return again and again to the truth I first learned as a boy: community is what saves us.

But Brookline also planted seeds of conflict. By the time I reached adulthood, I could feel the cracks forming between who I was expected to be and who I was becoming. The Catholic boy was supposed to follow a narrow path—Mass on Sundays, marriage within the faith, unquestioning obedience to church teaching. Yet the man I was becoming felt called to something wider, something that embraced not only the traditions of my childhood but also the resilience of my Jewish neighbors.

I didn't yet know how those two pieces of me would collide. I didn't know how costly that collision would one day be. But I knew enough to recognize that my story would not be confined to one lane. Brookline had given me both a foundation and a question mark. Looking back now, I can see the boy chasing

Eddie the Ice Cream King's truck down the street, GI Joes lined up in the dirt for battle, the street hockey games that stretched long past sunset. I can see the young man watching Jewish families celebrate Shabbat while he prepares for Sunday Mass. And I can hear the quiet whisper that began to stir inside me even then: these worlds are not so far apart.

Chapter 2

Faith at the Crossroads — Identity in Question

Faith is supposed to give us certainty, but for me, it gave me questions.

By the time I was a teenager, I had walked the Catholic path long enough to know its rhythms by heart. The Mass responses, the prayers, the incense-filled rituals—they were second nature. The act of kneeling, crossing myself, repeating the words in unison with hundreds of others became as automatic as tying my shoes. And yet, in the quiet spaces between ritual and reality, I found myself restless. My Catholic upbringing had built a sturdy frame, but something inside me kept looking outward.

That restlessness always seemed to circle back to the Jewish world around me.

In Brookline, Judaism wasn't an idea from a textbook—it was everywhere. It was the mezuzah nailed to a slant on a neighbor's doorframe. It was Hebrew songs drifting from the open window of the community center on a spring evening. It was the bakery on Harvard Street, where the smell of challah spilled into the air every Friday afternoon, golden braids stacked behind the glass like treasure. It was the synagogue parking lots packed on High Holidays, while I was at home sneaking a video game before Sunday Mass. Catholicism was my inheritance, but Judaism was my fascination.

Part of that fascination wasn't abstract at all—it was personal. Sometime in middle school, I fell in love for the first time. She was Jewish. I won't use her name, because that's not the point. The point is that for the first time, my curiosity about Judaism wasn't just shaped by history lessons or synagogue windows. It had a face. It had a smile. It had a laugh that made my stomach twist and my heart race in a way Mass never did.

We never dated—this was middle school, after all—but we talked, we sat near each other, we walked home the same way sometimes. And in those small interactions, something shifted in me. I wasn't just seeing Judaism from the outside anymore. I was drawn into it, not through doctrine, but through connection. My feelings for her faded with time, as childhood crushes do, but the spark she lit stayed with me. It was a reminder that my draw toward Judaism wasn't only intellectual—it was emotional, even spiritual.

That draw only deepened when I got my first job freshman year of high school—working at Morgan's Pharmacy. The place was just around the corner from Maimonides School, the modern Orthodox Jewish day school. Every afternoon, the store filled with kids in kippahs and skirts, dropping in to grab candy or toiletries before heading home. I was the one ringing them up, stocking the shelves, handing back their change. At first it was just a job, something to earn a little pocket money. But it became something more.

Those kids weren't just classmates from the periphery—they became part of my daily rhythm. Some of them joked with me, testing their English slang. Others were shy, mumbling "thank you" as they clutched candy bars. Some were bold enough to haggle over a pack of gum like it was a stock exchange deal. I watched them flood in together, laughing, arguing, teasing, but always with an energy that felt different from the Catholic kids I grew up with.

Sometimes I'd catch snatches of Hebrew between them. Other times I'd hear talk of holidays—Purim costumes, Pesach cleaning, Yom Kippur fasting. It wasn't from a book, or a teacher, or a ceremony—it was real life. Judaism wasn't something distant; it was alive, spilling over the counter every day in the form of kids chasing candy and sodas.

Working at Morgan's gave me a front-row seat to something simpler than history lessons or theology—just kids being kids. Every afternoon, the store became a kind of crossroads. Catholic kids from the neighborhood and kids from Maimonides, all chasing the same things: candy, baseball cards, magazines. I rang up Bazooka gum and Snickers bars, handed back quarters, and watched kids in Bruins hats laugh alongside kids in yarmulkes. Grandmothers with Irish brogues might be waiting in line behind Orthodox mothers in headscarves, both just picking up prescriptions or a few small things.

There were no speeches, no debates—just the everyday business of life. In those moments, the invisible lines between us didn't matter. Behind the counter, I saw two worlds that were supposed to be separate come together over Kit Kats and Mars bars, trading jokes and teasing one another like any group of kids. It wasn't profound at the time, but it stuck with me: the normalcy of it, the way differences seemed to fade in the glow of the candy racks.

I didn't always have the words for it, but I could feel it. My Catholic upbringing had taught me discipline and ritual. Working behind the counter at Morgan's, I saw another kind of glue holding people together—heritage, belonging, memory. That corner pharmacy became as much a classroom as my high school hallways.

Part of it was the weight of history. At school I learned about the Holocaust in detached textbook terms—dates, numbers, battle names. But when I talked to Jewish classmates and watched the kids from Maimonides, I realized this wasn't "history" for them. It was a memory. It lived in their families, in the way grandparents dodged questions about childhood, in the sharp way parents emphasized education, in the urgency of identity that pulsed just beneath the surface. Where my family spoke with pride about America, sport, or grandparents who had worked the docks, Jewish families spoke of exile, persecution, and survival. Both carried wounds, but the Jewish wounds felt older, deeper, rawer.

One memory in particular never left me. A Jewish friend mentioned, almost casually, that his grandmother still had the tattoo from Auschwitz on her arm. He said it the way a kid might mention that his grandfather had served in Korea—just a fact about the family. But to me, it was staggering. I had seen pictures of those tattoos in history books, grainy black-and-white photographs of gaunt figures behind barbed wire. To think that a grandmother in Brookline, living blocks from me, carried that same mark on her skin made the horror immediate. The Holocaust wasn't something that had ended in 1945. It was here, alive, living quietly in the homes of people I knew.

I couldn't shake that realization.

And it wasn't just the Holocaust. It was how Jewish life carried itself in everyday moments. Some of my friends were observant, keeping kosher, walking to synagogue. Others were secular, treating Judaism as more culture than religion. But all of them carried Jewishness as something non-negotiable. You could doubt God, you could wrestle with faith, you could even skip synagogue, but you were still a Jew. That permanence fascinated me.

In Catholicism, belief was everything. To doubt openly was dangerous—it marked you as faithless. In Judaism, belonging was everything. Doubt was almost expected, even embraced. A Catholic who questioned too much risked drifting outside the circle; a Jew who questioned was still firmly inside. I envied that permanence, that sense of identity that couldn't be stripped away by disbelief.

I started to notice how Jewish identity wasn't confined to the synagogue. It spilled into daily life. It was in the humor, sharp and self-aware. It was in the music, both celebratory and mournful. It was in the way parents spoke with urgency about education, about security, about passing something on. I realized that while Catholicism had taught me discipline and morality, Judaism seemed to offer resilience and continuity.

The more I saw, the more I felt drawn in.

But being drawn in wasn't simple. It created a quiet conflict inside me. At Sunday school, teachers spoke with a kind of finality about Jews: they had rejected Christ, they were blind to the truth. I never bought into the hostility, but I also didn't know how to reconcile the teaching with the people I knew. The Jewish kids I grew up with weren't blind—they were alive, vibrant, fiercely connected to something I could only admire.

It forced me to ask questions no teacher had prepared me for: What if the story I was taught wasn't the only way to see God? What if there was more than one path to truth? What if the very people my faith tradition framed as incomplete were actually the ones carrying the oldest truth of all?

I didn't share these thoughts widely. Doubt wasn't welcomed in Sunday school classrooms. Questions were tolerated only if they led back to the "right" answer. So I kept most of it inside, sorting through it silently, testing the bridge between what I had inherited and what I was discovering.

One of the most powerful realizations came not in a classroom but on the streets of Brookline. Every year, I would see gatherings around Holocaust remembrance. Survivors would speak, community leaders would read names of the dead, candles would be lit. I attended some of these events, drawn partly out of curiosity and partly out of respect. What struck me wasn't just the grief, but the determination.

These weren't memorials meant only to mourn—they were calls to vigilance. The message was clear: we will not forget, and we will not let it happen again.

That kind of collective willpower imprinted itself on me. It was different from Catholic rituals of remembrance, which often felt detached, almost otherworldly. Jewish remembrance was rooted in survival, in this world, in the idea that history had to be guarded or it would repeat itself.

By the time I left my teenage years, I knew I wasn't going to abandon Catholicism overnight. It was too deeply part of me—my family, my culture, my upbringing. But I also knew I couldn't unsee what I had seen in Judaism. I couldn't unhear the stories of survival, unfeel the weight of their resilience, and unlearn the permanence of belonging. The bridge was already there, and I was already walking it.

That bridge shaped how I saw everything that came after. In the military, when I found myself in places torn by ethnic and religious conflict, it was the Jewish story that gave me a frame for understanding survival. In rallies decades later, when I stood with a flag of Israel in my hand, it was the Jewish spirit that gave me courage. And in the darkest moments, when betrayal and injustice closed in, it was the memory of those survivors—their numbers etched on arms, their faith carried through fire—that reminded me I could endure too.

Brookline had introduced me to Judaism. But it was my own searching heart that built the bridge.

And once I started walking, there was no turning back.

Chapter 3:
Marching Into Uniform — Duty Over Self

Patriotism wasn't something I discovered late in life. It was something that grew in me from boyhood, shaped by stories of sacrifice, survival, and resilience. Growing up in Brookline, surrounded by Irish-Catholic tradition and the Jewish struggle for identity, I came to see freedom not as something guaranteed but as something fragile—something you defend or lose.

By the time I was a young man, the pull to serve was undeniable. The Cold War had ended, but the world wasn't stable. The Balkans were erupting in bloodshed, and America remained the nation others looked to when violence threatened to consume entire peoples. I didn't want to sit on the sidelines. I wanted to prove myself, to test the edges of who I was, to step into something larger than Brookline's narrow streets.

For me, that meant one thing: the United States Army.

The decision to enlist wasn't made in a single moment. It was the product of restlessness, of wanting a direction more purposeful than just working a job and watching the days slide by. The Army offered structure, identity, and a mission. I wanted all of that.

When I told my family, the reactions were mixed. Some admired the decision—proud that I was stepping up, proud that I was willing to wear the uniform. Others worried. They knew the Army wasn't just about discipline and benefits—it was about risk, about being sent to places where violence wasn't theoretical. But once the decision was made, I felt a strange calm. I had no illusions that it would be easy, but I believed it would be worth it.

What I didn't yet understand was just how completely the Army would strip me down and rebuild me, starting with the summer of my life at Fort Benning, Georgia.

Fort Benning in the summer is a world unto itself. Georgia heat doesn't just hang in the air—it crushes you. The sun bakes the red clay until it radiates upward, cooking you from the ground as the sky scorches you from above. The humidity wraps around you like a wet blanket, making every breath feel heavy, every movement sluggish. Add in the constant swarm of gnats and mosquitoes, and you quickly realize the South has its own way of testing your resolve.

It was there, in that furnace, that my transformation from civilian to soldier began.

The first days were a blur of shouting drill sergeants, endless paperwork, and the sudden realization that individuality was gone. You weren't "Scott Hayes" anymore. You were "Private Hayes." You weren't allowed to stand apart—you moved, ate, breathed as part of a group. If one man screwed up, all paid the price. The message was clear: there was no "I" in the Army.

Mornings started before dawn, the heat already rising from the ground like steam. The sound of boots on gravel, barked commands, and the metallic clatter of equipment filled the air. Physical training meant push-ups in the mud, running in formation until lungs burned, obstacle courses that left skin raw and muscles screaming. The Georgia sun made every exercise twice as punishing. By 9 a.m., uniforms were soaked through with sweat, salt staining the fabric.

Fort Benning had a way of humbling you. No matter how tough you thought you were, the combination of heat, exhaustion, and relentless discipline broke you down. That was the point. The Army wasn't interested in who you had been before. It wanted to tear you apart and build you into something new: a soldier.

Meals were rushed, swallowed in minutes at the mess hall before you were herded back outside. Sleep was rationed, rarely more than a few hours before reveille jolted you awake. Showers were quick, with no privacy. Letters from home were read under fluorescent lights, then shoved into duffel bags before lights-out. Every detail of life was regimented, timed, and enforced.

At first, I resisted. Everyone does. You cling to your sense of self, to the idea that you're still the same person who walked in. But the heat, the sweat, the endless drills chip away at that. Slowly, the resistance fades. You stop thinking about yourself and start thinking about the unit. You stop asking "why me?" and start asking "how do we get through this?"

And in that shift, something powerful happens: brotherhood.

The Army forged bonds I had never known before. In the sweltering Georgia heat, we became more than recruits—we became brothers. Different races, religions, and hometowns blurred into one as we endured the same punishment together. The drill sergeants broke us as individuals, but in that breaking, they created something stronger.

I remember standing in formation, sweat dripping into my eyes, knees shaking from exhaustion, and looking left and right at men who were just as drained, just as battered, but still standing. That look—that unspoken acknowledgment—was where trust was born. You didn't have to like the man next to you, but you knew he would carry your pack if you collapsed. You knew you would do the same for him.

That trust became a lifeline. It was what got us through forced marches, through endless hours on the firing range, through nights when the air was so thick with humidity you felt like you were drowning just lying in your bunk.

The discipline drilled into us at Fort Benning echoed lessons I had first seen in faith communities. Catholic rituals had taught me repetition, order, obedience. Jewish neighbors had taught me resilience, the value of continuity under pressure. But the Army sharpened both lessons into survival skills.

When a drill sergeant screamed an order, hesitation wasn't an option. Delay could mean death in combat. When a fellow soldier stumbled, you didn't step around him—you lifted him, because your own life might depend on him tomorrow. Discipline wasn't just about following rules. It was about creating reflexes that would keep you alive.

As summer bled into fall, training shifted from raw endurance to preparation for the real world. We weren't just learning how to march and shoot—we were being shaped into soldiers who could be sent anywhere on earth. Rumors spread through the barracks about where we'd go next. Some guys prayed for stateside posts, others dreamed of Korea or Hawaii.

When my name was called, the Drill Sergeant looked at his clipboard and barked a word that made my stomach leap: *Germany.* Not just anywhere in Germany—Baumholder.

Baumholder wasn't a household name, but in the Army it carried weight. Perched in the hills of the Rhineland, it had been a U.S. Army post since the end of World War II. Soldiers stationed there had stood guard through the Cold War, training in mud, snow, and endless field exercises. It was known as one of the toughest posts in Europe, with a reputation for hard conditions and harder training.

And then there was the unit: the 1st Armored Division. "Old Ironsides." A division forged in World War II, carrying honors from North Africa, Anzio, and beyond. It had stared down the Soviets in Germany and rolled through Desert Storm. To wear that patch was to inherit decades of grit and sacrifice.

For me, it felt almost like fate. Back at Brookline High, as a freshman, I had chosen German instead of Spanish or French. Most of my friends thought it was a strange choice, but I liked the sound of the language, the challenge of its grammar, and the way it opened a window to a country I had only read about in history books. I never imagined that one day the Army would stamp *Germany* on my orders and ship me straight into that world—not as a student, but as a soldier.

That night in the barracks, I lay awake thinking about it. I imagined the forests and the castles, the cobblestone streets, the echoes of history. I thought about all the soldiers before me who had passed through Baumholder, carrying the same nerves and anticipation. For the first time, I felt the Army was sending me somewhere that mattered—not just a post, but a place with history in its soil.

My time in Germany gave me countless experiences I could never have predicted, but one stands above the rest. In November 1995, I sat down to Thanksgiving dinner with President Bill Clinton, First Lady Hillary Clinton, and German Chancellor Helmut Kohl.

It was surreal. One moment I was just another young soldier stationed overseas, missing home and the comforts of an American holiday. Next, I was in a dining hall where the Commander-in-Chief himself was shaking hands, serving food, and reminding us that we weren't forgotten. Hillary Clinton was gracious, speaking to soldiers like we were old friends. Chancellor Kohl, towering and statesmanlike, represented the bridge between our two nations—Germany rising from its past, America standing as its guarantor of freedom.

For a kid from Brookline, who had once stocked shelves at Morgan's Pharmacy and chased Eddie the Ice Cream King down the street, it was almost impossible to believe. Thanksgiving had always been about family gatherings, football on TV, and plates of turkey at home. That year, my "family" was the Army, and my tablemates were the leader of the free world and the leader of Germany.

That dinner was more than a meal—it was a reminder of why I had enlisted. Service wasn't abstract. It wasn't just drills in the Georgia heat. It connected you to something larger: the defense of freedom, the bonds between nations, the thread of history that ran from Brookline to Baumholder, from the classrooms of Brookline High to the halls of power in Washington and Berlin.

Baumholder wasn't just a post—it was a world unto itself. The training areas stretched for miles, rugged and unforgiving, with rolling hills that seemed designed to break you down. None were more infamous than the *Ball Buster Hills.* The name said it all. Steep, relentless inclines that turned PT into pure punishment. We ran them over and over, lungs burning, legs shaking, sweat pouring down in the cold German air. At the top, there was no victory—just the knowledge that the Sergeant would send us down again. But the hills forged endurance, both physical and mental. If you could survive the Ball Busters, you could survive anything.

The days were long, but the nights offered their own rhythm. Soldiers needed release, and Baumholder had its outlets. The *Rod and Gun Club* was a staple—a place where soldiers gathered to blow off steam, share stories, and forget, at least for a few hours, the weight of training and the distance from home. Cigarette smoke curled through the air, beer mugs clinked, and laughter rolled as loud as the jukebox. Deals were made over pool tables, rivalries born over dartboards. It wasn't glamorous, but it was ours.

Then there was *Kelly's Irish Pub* downtown, a little taste of home for someone like me. It had the charm of a dive bar, with its dim lighting, sticky floors, and bartenders who knew enough English to keep the drinks flowing. Soldiers from every corner of America crowded in alongside locals, and for a few hours, uniforms and ranks didn't matter. Kelly's was where you could sit shoulder-to-shoulder with someone you'd cursed at during formation that morning and laugh over a pint by nightfall. It was where stories were traded, girlfriends were bragged about, and homesickness was dulled by Guinness.

Between the punishing PT and the long nights in the clubs and pubs, Baumholder etched itself into me. It wasn't the glamorous posting some soldiers dreamed of, but it gave me a sense of belonging. It toughened me, bonded me to my brothers in arms, and reminded me daily that service was about more than drills or orders. It was about carrying each other—up Ball Buster Hills, through the smoke-filled nights of the Rod and Gun Club, and into the uncertain future we all knew was coming.

Chapter 4:

Shadows Over Bosnia — Witness to Division

The Army had trained me to be a soldier. Bosnia taught me what that actually meant.

When I first arrived, the air itself felt heavy. It wasn't just the weight of a new country or the exhaustion of deployment—it was the silence of a land that had been torn apart. Bosnia was a place where hatred had soaked into the soil. Every street, every hillside, seemed to carry scars: buildings reduced to shells, villages burned out, grave markers rising in fields where children once played.

I had studied conflict in classrooms, watched it on television, trained for it in the Georgia heat. But nothing could prepare me for standing in a place where neighbors had turned on neighbors, where ethnic cleansing wasn't a term in a policy paper—it was something you could see in the eyes of survivors.

I was on one of the first plane loads of troops into Bosnia. We flew in on a C-130, packed shoulder-to-shoulder, the hum of the engines drowning out any attempt at sleep. When the crew chief shouted for us to prepare for landing, it wasn't the smooth descent of a commercial flight. This was a tactical landing. The aircraft dropped fast, banking hard, the kind of maneuver designed to keep us from being easy targets. My stomach lurched as the plane seemed to fall out of the sky, then slammed onto the runway with a bone-rattling jolt.

It was early morning, the kind of gray dawn where the light feels thin and uncertain. The rear ramp dropped, and before the smell of jet fuel had even cleared, we were being hustled off the tarmac. Word came quickly: there were fears of incoming fire, and the Air Force didn't want us sitting ducks on the runway. We moved fast, rifles slung, packs digging into our shoulders, hearts pounding from adrenaline and the sudden cold slap of Balkan air.

Our first stop was an old concrete hangar, a relic of a different era, its walls cracked and scarred. That would be our staging ground. There, we unloaded gear, erected our GP medium tent, and tried to carve out a corner of order in a land that felt anything but orderly. The ground was frozen, our breath hung in the air, and the reality of deployment settled in. This wasn't Fort Benning. This wasn't Baumholder. This was a country fresh out of war.

Before long, our assignment came down: guard duty. We would be manning a section of the wire, rotating through a bunker that overlooked the perimeter. From the outside, it looked like just another coil of barbed wire cutting through mud and snow. But on the inside, we knew it was a line between fragile peace and the chaos still lingering beyond. Sitting in that bunker, eyes scanning the treeline, every sound seemed amplified—the snap of branches, the crunch of boots in the snow, the low growl of engines in the distance.

That first day taught me more than months of training ever could. The Army had given me the skills, but Bosnia gave me the context. We weren't preparing for war anymore. We were in it, living in the uneasy silence of a land where peace had to be guarded at gunpoint.

Life in Bosnia quickly settled into a rhythm that was equal parts monotony and sudden tension. Our primary job at first was guard duty—rotating shifts on the wire and in the bunkers that ringed the airfield. The days blurred into nights, the cold seeping into your bones no matter how many layers you wore.

We improvised to survive it. One of the best tricks was taking a .50 caliber ammo can, filling it with sand, then pouring in diesel. Once lit, it became a makeshift stove. The flames would lick just high enough to keep your hands from freezing, the smell of burning diesel mixing with the crisp bite of Balkan air. We'd huddle around it during the long watches, trading stories in low voices, trying to ignore how much time was left in our shift.

Facilities were primitive. The outhouses were little more than plywood boxes, and the job nobody envied was burning the waste with diesel once the drums were full. The smell was unforgettable, acrid smoke curling through the camp, clinging to your uniform no matter how hard you tried to shake it.

Even the hangar we first used as cover carried its own dangers. Not long after setting up, we learned the perimeter of the structure had been daisy-chained with MRUD anti-personnel mines—Yugoslav-made cousins of the Claymore. They were leftovers from whoever had occupied it last. That discovery sent a chill through all of us. We were sleeping, eating, and working in a place designed to kill. The reality of Bosnia set in deeper: even the ground beneath your boots couldn't be trusted.

Meals were the standard Army MREs—nothing fancy, but they kept you going. Over time, you developed favorites. Mine were chicken and rice, and meatballs with beef and rice in spicy tomato sauce. They weren't gourmet, but when you'd been sitting in a frozen bunker for hours, tearing open that brown plastic pouch felt like Christmas. Soldiers traded entrees like kids traded baseball cards, and you always knew who had scored a pack with a coveted pound cake inside.

Not every moment was routine. Guarding the main gate to Tuzla Airfield, I had one encounter that has stayed with me. A man walked by—a jihadi, or at least someone who wanted us to think he was. He looked directly at us, drew his finger across his throat in a slow, deliberate motion, then kept walking. He didn't run. He didn't hide. He just wanted us to know he was there, that the hatred outside the wire wasn't going away. I kept my rifle at the ready, watching his back as he disappeared down the road, the gesture burning itself into my memory.

That was Bosnia: long stretches of boredom broken by moments of unease, sometimes terror. One minute you were stomping your feet to stay warm by a makeshift diesel heater, the next you were reminded—by mines underfoot or a throat-cutting gesture—that death was never far away.

The children of Bosnia were the hardest part. No amount of training prepared you for them. On patrol, they would run out to wave, chasing our vehicles, smiling with a brightness that seemed impossible in the ruins around them. Sometimes they begged for food, sometimes just for attention. We gave what we could—MRE crackers, candy, bottled water—but what they really wanted was something we couldn't give: safety.

I remember one girl, maybe eight years old, holding her little brother's hand as she stood by the roadside. Their clothes were worn thin, their faces smudged with dust, but their eyes followed us with a mix of hope and fear. It was the same look I had seen in pictures of Jewish children during the Holocaust—wide-eyed, desperate for rescue, uncertain if rescue would ever come. That memory lodged in my heart and never left.

But the kids weren't just symbols of innocence—they were also part of the daily barter economy that soldiers stumbled into. When our rations got old and the taste of MREs wore thin, we found ourselves trading with local kids. A pack of peanut butter crackers or a pouch of instant coffee could get you a loaf of fresh bread, still warm from an oven. Sometimes it was cevapi—little grilled sausages stuffed into bread with onions—that tasted like heaven compared to freeze-dried meat. Other times, when our tobacco ran out, a kid would produce a handful of local cigarettes in exchange for candy or a packet of matches.

It wasn't official, and it certainly wasn't by the book, but it was human. These kids lived in a warzone, scavenging whatever scraps they could. We were soldiers, tired of eating from brown plastic pouches, desperate for even a bite of normal life. The trades were simple, wordless half the time, but they reminded us of something bigger: that even in the rubble of hate, people still reached for connection, for survival, for a moment of dignity.

Those children stayed with me more than any briefing or patrol log ever could. Their laughter, their bartering, even their cautious smiles—all of it cut through the bleakness. They were living proof that life pushed forward, no matter how much destruction tried to hold it back.

Bosnia wasn't just rubble and refugees. It was also simmering hostility, hatred so thick you could feel it in the air. On some patrols, we intercepted groups of armed men—paramilitaries who claimed to be "protecting their people" but were really sowing terror. Weapons caches turned up in barns, ammunition buried in fields, hidden away like seeds waiting for the next harvest of violence. Peace was supposed to have been signed, but the war hadn't ended—it had only shifted shape.

The stories we heard, and the sights we saw, carried echoes of something I had first learned about in Brookline classrooms: the Holocaust. Bosnia wasn't genocide on that scale, but it had the same poison in its veins. The siege of Sarajevo was the most chilling example. For nearly four years, Serb forces surrounded the city, shelling civilians daily, snipers picking off men, women, and even children who dared to cross open streets. Over ten thousand people died, most of them civilians. The photographs of emaciated prisoners behind barbed wire, the skeletal remains uncovered in mass graves—it was impossible not to think of Auschwitz, of Bergen-Belsen, of the black-and-white images I had studied in school.

Only now, it wasn't history. It was happening in my lifetime, in the same continent where Jews had been slaughtered fifty years earlier. The hatred was the same; the target was just different. One generation had killed in the name of racial purity; another was killing in the name of ethnic and religious supremacy.

And it wasn't just the Serbs or Croats. Bosnia had become a magnet for foreign fighters—Islamic jihadis who poured in from the Middle East, North Africa, even as far away as Afghanistan. They saw the Bosnian war as their chance for jihad, to spill blood in the name of God. We heard whispers of them in villages, saw their long beards and foreign dress, and caught glimpses of them moving in the shadows. Some carried themselves like veterans hardened in Afghanistan, others were young and reckless, desperate for martyrdom. They weren't there to protect—they were there to inflame.

That was Bosnia: neighbors turning on neighbors, fueled by outside forces eager to exploit old wounds. It was hatred passed down like an heirloom, sharpened by propaganda, and sanctified by men who twisted religion into a license for murder. I remember one village elder telling us flatly that he would never forgive his neighbors. He said it the way another man might say he was planting corn in spring—with certainty, without hesitation.

Listening to him, I couldn't help but feel the weight of history pressing down. I had grown up hearing "Never Again" in reference to the Holocaust. In Bosnia, I understood how fragile those words were. Never Again wasn't a promise—it was a battle, one that had to be fought over and over, in every generation, against every form of hatred that rose from the ashes.

After weeks at Tuzla Airfield, our orders shifted. We packed up and moved deeper into Bosnia, toward the town of Kladanj. If Tuzla had felt fragile, Kladanj felt raw. Our new "camp" wasn't much more than a muddy field when we arrived—uneven ground churned by trucks, patches of ice clinging stubbornly where the sun never reached.

At first, we set up GP medium tents in the muck, pounding stakes into ground that seemed determined to swallow them whole. Mud coated everything: our boots, our cots, even the gear inside the tents. When it rained, the field turned into a swamp, sucking at your steps, pooling under the canvas floors so that you woke up with damp socks no matter how carefully you stacked your belongings.

But slowly, as soldiers do, we carved order out of chaos. Engineers came in with conex containers, stacking them into makeshift housing. We laid down gravel paths to cut through the mud, and by degrees the swamp became something resembling a camp. The real luxury came later—hot showers. After weeks of baby wipes and cold water in canteens, stepping into a steaming shower felt like civilization had finally caught up with us. The first time the hot water hit my skin, I could have wept from relief.

Not all of our time was spent in the tents. Some rotations had us stationed at an abandoned UN base in Kladanj. The place had the ghostly feel of a halfway house between order and collapse. Faded blue helmets were still stenciled on walls, empty bunks lined the barracks, and half-forgotten paperwork littered the offices. You could almost feel the presence of the peacekeepers who had been there before us, caught in the same uneasy role of trying to hold back a tide of hatred with little more than wire fences and good intentions.

We did what soldiers always do: made the best of it. The abandoned base gave us sturdier walls, better shelter, and the eerie reminder that we were not the first to try and hold this ground. The silence in those hallways was thick, as if the building itself carried the weight of what it had seen—soldiers leaving in a hurry, civilians seeking refuge, maybe even gunfire echoing in the hills outside.

Kladanj never became comfortable, but it became familiar. The mud, the tents, the conex boxes, even the borrowed bones of a UN camp—they were the backdrop of our lives. It was there, in that patch of Bosnia, that we learned how to create a sense of "home" in the middle of a place that had been stripped of it.

Service in Bosnia wasn't glorious. It wasn't the kind of service you tell war stories about at a bar. It was grueling, frustrating, morally complex. There were no clean victories, no simple endings. We weren't there to win—we were there to hold the line, to keep the fragile peace from collapsing altogether.

I was only nineteen. Nineteen years old and standing in a place where the worst of humanity had left its mark. The Army had trained me to march, to shoot, to follow orders. It had not trained me to look into a shallow pit and see the outline of bodies where children once played. It hadn't trained me to stand in villages where neighbors had butchered each other, where burned-out homes stood as silent witnesses to betrayal. We called it ethnic cleansing. The words sounded clinical, almost bureaucratic. But in Bosnia, ethnic cleansing wasn't an idea—it was a smell, a sight, a silence that never left you.

And it wasn't just one side. Both Serbs and Bosniaks had blood on their hands. Some villages bore the scars of Serb campaigns; others carried the evidence of revenge carried out by Bosnian militias. Hatred didn't discriminate—it consumed everyone it touched. For a nineteen-year-old kid from

Brookline, raised on GI Joes and flashlight tag, it was like stepping into another world. One where the rules of childhood no longer applied, where the "bad guys" weren't wearing uniforms and the "good guys" weren't always innocent.

The images stayed with me long after the patrols ended. At night, I would lie in my bunk in Kladanj or Tuzla, staring up at the tent ceiling, sleep refusing to come. My mind replayed the faces of children on the roadside, the emptiness of burned homes, the hollow stares of survivors who had lost everything. Some nights it was the smell that haunted me—the acrid bite of burned villages or the unmistakable odor of death when mass graves were uncovered. Other nights, it was the sounds: distant gunfire echoing through hills, or the sudden quiet of a village where laughter had once lived.

There were moments I wanted to shut it out, to build walls inside myself. But the walls didn't hold. The memories seeped through. Bosnia branded itself on me in ways I didn't understand then, but would carry for the rest of my life.

And yet, for all the weight, I never doubted why we were there. Because when you stand at the edge of a mass grave at nineteen years old, you understand the stakes. You understand that words like "Never Again" aren't slogans—they're responsibilities.

When my rotation in Bosnia ended, I returned to Germany in October of 1996, just under a year after I had first deployed. Coming back felt surreal. Bosnia had aged me in ways I couldn't yet name, and stepping off the transport into Baumholder was like being dropped into another universe. The mud, the mass graves, the haunted eyes of refugees—all of it was behind me, and yet it was still inside me. Germany felt like a reprieve, but also a reminder that the Army doesn't pause for your memories.

Life snapped back to its rhythms: shining boots until they gleamed like mirrors, pressing uniforms so sharp they could cut, and dragging myself out of bed before dawn for PT. The Ball Buster Hills hadn't gone anywhere. They still loomed above Baumholder like cruel guardians, and running them again felt like penance and rebirth all at once. Every incline brought Bosnia back to mind, but it also grounded me, reminded me that no matter what I'd seen, I was still a soldier—and the job demanded discipline.

But Germany wasn't only about duty. It was also where my life took a turn I never could have planned. One night around Halloween, I found myself back at Kelly's Irish Pub downtown—the same smoky dive where soldiers and locals mixed, where Guinness and laughter dulled the edge of homesickness. The place was packed, costumes here and there, the music loud, the air thick with cigarette smoke and the smell of spilled beer.

Somewhere between the noise and the drinks, I found myself talking to her. She was German, sharp-eyed, and unimpressed by soldiers' usual lines. On a dare—or maybe just on impulse—I let someone draw a heart on my cheek in lipstick. I leaned in and asked her to kiss it. She didn't miss a beat. She looked me dead in the eye and called me an asshole.

I laughed, partly out of embarrassment and partly because I knew she wasn't wrong. What I didn't know at that moment was that the woman who brushed me off in Kelly's that night would one day become my wife.

The weeks after that night didn't follow a straight path. There were conversations, some stilted, some effortless. There were cultural barriers—my broken German, her amused tolerance of my mistakes. But something grew between us. Slowly, in a town full of soldiers looking for distraction, I found someone who was different. Someone who didn't just see the uniform, but saw me.

Back in Baumholder, my days were filled with the Army grind—PT, inspections, long field exercises. But at night, when the boots were off and the uniform hung in the locker, I had something else. A reason to stay, a reason to look forward, a reason to believe that even in the shadow of war and discipline, life could build something new.

Bosnia 2.0

Two years after my first deployment, I found myself back in Bosnia. It was 1998, and the country I returned to was not the same Bosnia I had left behind in 1996. The war's raw edges had begun to dull, the ceasefire held firmer, and the chaos that had once hung over every patrol had given way to something resembling stability.

But "better" didn't mean easy.

We were stationed at Camp Bedrock, a base on the outskirts of Tuzla. Home was still a GP Medium tent—canvas stretched tight against the wind, cots lined up in rows, duffel bags doubling as closets. Even after years of NATO presence, this wasn't luxury. Mud still crept into everything. The cold still cuts through your layers. And nights were still long, with the hum of generators and the distant echoes of a country not yet healed.

Unlike my first deployment, there were no Bradleys this time. The armored beasts that had made us feel like mobile fortresses in 1995 were gone. Now we rode in up-armored Humvees, their canvas doors and thin metal bodies offering little more than the illusion of protection. Rolling out of the gate, you felt exposed in a way that was hard to put into words. Bosnia might have been calmer, but it wasn't harmless. Every pothole could hide a mine, every bend in the road could conceal an ambush.

The difference was visible everywhere. Villages were rebuilt. Markets reopened with stalls selling fruit, bread, and cigarettes. Children played soccer in streets that had once been deserted. There were still scars—burned-out buildings, grave markers on hillsides, neighbors who refused to speak to one another—but there was also life creeping back into the ruins.

For us, the mission shifted too. Less combat readiness, more presence. We were there to remind the factions that peace still had teeth, that NATO's eyes were always watching. Patrols meant long hours on the road, stopping to talk with locals, monitoring checkpoints, and showing the flag. There were fewer confrontations, but the tension never fully disappeared. It hung in the background, a reminder that hatred doesn't vanish overnight—it waits, patient and quiet, for its chance to flare again.

Daily life blurred into a routine. PT in the mornings, guard shifts on the perimeter, patrols through the countryside. Meals still came in the form of MREs more often than we liked, though sometimes the locals traded us fresh bread or grilled meat, reminders of normal life. Letters from home were read and reread until the paper grew soft, and the rare phone call felt like a lifeline.

At Camp Bedrock, we learned to make do. We built little comforts where we could—a deck of cards passed around, a radio pulling in scratchy music, someone's care package of beef jerky becoming currency. Nights meant stories swapped under the canvas roof, laughter covering fatigue, and sometimes silence when the memories of 1995 crept back.

Bosnia in 1998 was different, but so was I. I was no longer the nineteen-year-old kid shocked by his first glimpse of mass graves. I had carried those memories, and they had hardened into something else: perspective. The mission wasn't glamorous, but it mattered. The absence of war was fragile, and it was our job to hold it together.

Looking back, Bosnia 2.0 wasn't about firefights or danger. It was about presence, patience, and persistence. It was about proving that peace could be more than a pause between wars. And for me, it was another reminder that wearing the uniform wasn't just about fighting enemies—it was about standing guard over humanity itself.

Chapter 5:
Kosovo's Dividing Lines — Boundaries of Blood

Kosovo was where war became a repetition.

By the time I first deployed there, I already had Bosnia etched into my memory: burned-out villages, children on the roadside, the raw edge of hatred that never seemed to die. Kosovo was different in some ways, but the ghosts were the same.

The road to Kosovo started with a C-130. We flew into Skopje, Macedonia, landing at a UN base that was already crowded with soldiers, vehicles, and the endless churn of logistics. Compared to Bosnia, where my first deployment had begun with a tactical landing and fears of incoming fire, this arrival felt steady, if not routine. No alarms, no sprinting off a runway—just the steady thrum of engines and the knowledge that another mission was beginning.

From Skopje, we loaded into a convoy bound for Kosovo. The ride was long, the kind of movement that blurs together in your memory. Bradleys led the way—big, armored beasts that gave you a sense of security. But most of us rode in up-armored Humvees, their heavy metal doors offering more than a shell against the outside world. As the miles passed, we watched villages roll by—some battered, others stubbornly alive. The landscape was hilly, dotted with mosques and farms, the roads rough but navigable.

Hours later, we pulled into Camp Monteith in Gjilane, the town that would become our base of operations. Nothing about the arrival was dramatic. No firefights, no explosions—just the grind of soldiers dismounting, unloading gear, and setting up for yet another chapter of peacekeeping. But even in that ordinary convoy, there was a quiet weight. Everyone knew we weren't just passing through. We were here to stand between neighbors who had already shed blood, to guard borders that were more suggestion than reality.

Camp Monteith itself was a mix of prefab structures and tents, a place thrown together in a hurry but functional enough to serve as home. From there, we pushed out daily—patrolling Gjilane's streets, running border missions, and keeping watch on the neutral zone that divided Kosovo from Serbia. The war felt contained, but the air carried tension, the kind that told you peace was still fragile, still waiting for the wrong spark.

Our primary mission out of Camp Monteith was guarding the border with the neutral zone separating Kosovo from Serbia. On paper, it was supposed to be a buffer, a space where conflict couldn't spill across. In reality, it was a sieve. The UCPMB—the Liberation Army of Preševo, Medveđa and Bujanovac—was still active, slipping across with weapons, supplies, and fighters.

Most days were long stretches of monotony: staring at tree lines, scanning unpaved roads, keeping radios alive with static-filled chatter. But every so often, monotony cracked open into tension. We'd intercept small groups of armed men moving at night, or stumble on caches hidden under brush or stashed in vehicles. Rifles wrapped in tarps, crates of ammunition buried in shallow pits—reminders that the war wasn't gone, just waiting for its moment. Each find was like pulling a thread from a web, but we knew the web stretched wider than we could ever untangle.

The outposts along the border had to be manned no matter the conditions, and the roads that led there weren't kind. Mud in spring, dust in summer, ice and snow in winter. Being the only guy in my platoon from the Northeast—someone who actually knew how to handle snow—I got "gifted" the job nobody else wanted: driving the snowplow Humvee to clear the road to the border outpost.

That Humvee was built more for persistence than comfort. No armor, just a plow bolted on the front, chains rattling on the tires, and a heater that worked only when it felt like it. The road up was unpaved and unforgiving, winding with a steep drop on the passenger side. If you looked over the edge, you could see how far down you'd tumble if you lost control—and it wasn't a drop you'd walk away from.

I learned quickly to drive with the door open and my hand braced against it, seatbelt off. The idea was simple: if the Humvee started to slide, I'd bail. It wasn't exactly a safety manual technique, but it gave me a fighting chance. More than once, I felt the rear tires slip toward the edge, the whole vehicle tilting just enough to make my heart stop. Every time, I muscled it back, white-knuckled, the plow groaning as it pushed through snow and ice.

The guys used to laugh and say I was half-crazy, sitting there with the door open, ready to jump. But they also knew that without that plow clearing the road, nobody was getting to the outpost. It was one of those unglamorous jobs that didn't make reports or headlines, but it kept the mission moving.

That road became my personal battlefield—less about gunfire, more about gravity and ice. In its own way, it was just as dangerous.

Just as I was settling into a rhythm in Kosovo, the Army reminded me of a truth every soldier learns sooner or later: stability is an illusion. Orders come down when they come down, and your life changes with the stroke of a pen. Mine read: Fort Drum,

On paper, it was just a reassignment. In reality, it meant uprooting the life I had built over six years in Germany—a country I had grown to love.

When I returned to Baumholder to prepare for the move, the logistics hit me first. My wife needed a visa, which meant navigating endless paperwork, embassy visits, and the bureaucracy that always seemed to move at half speed when you needed it fast. At the same time, we had to pack up everything we owned—our furniture, keepsakes, the little nest we had built together—and prepare to ship it across the Atlantic.

But beneath the grind of forms and boxes, there was something heavier: sadness. Germany had stopped being just a duty station for me. It had become home. I loved the language I had struggled through, the food that had become comfort, the rhythm of German life. I had friends there, real friends, men and women who didn't see me just as "the American soldier" but as part of their circle. On Sundays, I played with a local soccer team, lacing up my cleats and running the pitch like any other guy in town. It was one of the few places I could forget rank, orders, or deployment and just be Scott. Leaving that behind felt like tearing out a piece of myself.

Packing day was the hardest. Each box sealed felt like closing a chapter. My wife felt it too—Germany was her country, her home, her family. For her, leaving wasn't just sad—it was sacrifice. She was stepping into a new world for me, one she hadn't chosen, one that would take her thousands of miles away from everything familiar.

The flight to the U.S. was quiet, not just because of exhaustion, but because we both knew what we were leaving behind. For six years, Germany had given me a sense of belonging, a second identity beyond the uniform. Now, the Army was asking me to trade that for the icy winds of upstate New York and whatever waited for us at Fort Drum.

After leaving Germany, we took some leave in Norwood, Massachusetts. For me, it was more than just downtime — it was the first chance in years to sit with my family, eat at familiar tables, and walk streets where I wasn't "Private" or "Specialist Hayes," just Scott again. But leave always goes fast, and soon enough we were loading up again, this time for the long drive north to Fort Drum.

Fort Drum was a different world. The North Country winters were brutal, far worse than anything even Baumholder had thrown at me. Snow piled high, the cold seeping into everything, the wind cutting through layers of uniform and gear. But the weather wasn't the only shock — the Army itself was different. I had spent my career so far in mechanized infantry, riding and fighting out of Bradleys. At Drum, I was suddenly in a light infantry unit. No armor to carry you, no steel beasts to back you up. Your legs were your vehicle. If you wanted to get somewhere, you rucked it with everything on your back.

That shift demanded a new mindset. The workouts were different, the expectations sharper. Marches were longer, gear felt heavier, and the pace never let up. I had to re-train my body and my head to think like a light fighter, to move quicker, endure more, and live without the protection of tracks and armor. It was humbling at first — I felt like I had to unlearn and relearn everything I thought I knew about being an infantryman. But soon enough, I adapted, because that's what soldiers do.

Just as I was finding my footing, history changed.

September 11

I was at Fort Polk, Louisiana, training with my unit for another deployment back to Kosovo, when the world turned upside down. Word spread through the training grounds in pieces — a plane had hit the World Trade Center, then another, then the Pentagon. At first, we didn't believe it. Everyone thought it was some kind of accident, a rumor blown out of proportion. But then the news confirmed it: America was under attack.

I remember the silence that fell over us once reality set in. Soldiers don't often go quiet, but that day we did. We gathered around radios and TVs, watching the towers burn and fall, watching people flee through the smoke, watching a kind of horror none of us thought we'd see on our own soil. For me, it was a gut punch. I had seen hatred tear apart Bosnia, watched it linger in Kosovo — but now that same hatred had struck home.

In that moment, everything changed. The training at Polk suddenly felt like it was aimed in the wrong direction. Kosovo was still on the books, but every one of us knew: this wasn't going to be the same Army, and these weren't going to be the same wars. The fight we had been training for overseas was now connected directly to the ashes in New York and Washington.

Kosovo 2.0

When the orders came down, I couldn't help but shake my head. Kosovo. Again. After all the moves, all the training, all the preparation, I was going back to the very same place, the very same town: Gjilan.

It was déjà vu from the moment I stepped off the transport. The same streets. The same faces. The same border roads leading into the neutral zone. Even the same church — the Serbian Orthodox church in town — that we were tasked with guarding against attacks. It was surreal, like rewinding a tape and pressing play again.

The work didn't change much either. Day after day, we patrolled Gjilan, showing presence, trying to keep the peace. We walked the same streets until I knew every crack in the pavement, every graffiti-marked wall. The same kids would run out to greet us, bold enough to ask for candy or gum. The same old men would sit on stoops, eyeing us with a mix of suspicion and resignation. Guarding the church became routine too —

long hours standing watch, making sure no one tried to torch it or deface it. It wasn't glamorous soldiering, but it mattered. The church was more than a building. It was a symbol. Protecting it meant showing that history couldn't just be erased overnight, no matter how deep the hatred ran.

But with each patrol, each guard shift, the weight of repetition settled heavier. Bosnia had felt urgent, raw. Kosovo 1.0 had felt tense, unstable. Kosovo 2.0 felt… stagnant. Like we were holding our breath, waiting for something to give, but never knowing if it would.

And then one day, it wasn't war that shook us — it was the earth itself.

I was sitting in a coffee shop when it started. At first I thought it was artillery in the distance, some muffled blast rolling through the ground. Then the floor rattled, cups slid off tables, the lights overhead swayed, and the air filled with a deep, groaning sound I'll never forget.

An earthquake.

In seconds, the whole town was alive with chaos. People rushed into the streets, shouting, clutching children, pointing at cracked buildings and falling plaster. The minaret of the mosque toppled, crumbling in a cloud of dust. Cars screeched to a stop. The ground beneath us kept rumbling, like the world itself had decided to remind us who was really in charge.

For soldiers trained to expect human threats — fighters slipping across the border, ambushes in the hills — there's no training for the earth itself rebelling. I remember standing outside, watching the pavement ripple, and feeling powerless in a way I never had in uniform. You can fight men. You can intercept weapons. You can guard a church. But you can't fight the ground shaking beneath your boots.

When it ended, silence returned — thick, eerie, heavier than the quake itself. We stepped into the streets alongside the locals, checking for damage, making sure no one was trapped. Some buildings had cracked, a few had partially collapsed, but most still stood. Still, the fear on people's faces was unmistakable. For civilians who had already lived through years of war and instability, the quake was just another reminder that nothing was guaranteed. Not safety, not homes, not even the ground they walked on.

For me, it was humbling. Kosovo had taught me about fragility before, but this was different. The quake made the repetition of our daily patrols feel almost absurd. We were guarding against the hatred of men, but nature could tear everything down in an instant. In a strange way, it connected me to the people we were there to protect. We shared the same helplessness, the same lesson: survival isn't guaranteed, not from enemies, not from the earth.

Looking back, my two deployments to Kosovo blur together in some ways. The patrols, the border duty, the children's smiles, the sudden flashes of violence—they form a mosaic of repetition. But in another sense, they stand apart.

The first deployment was about proving myself as a soldier. The second was about enduring as a man with something to lose—and realizing how fragile everything truly is, whether it's peace held together by foreign soldiers or earth that shakes without warning.

Kosovo taught me that service is never just about the mission. It's about the life you build in between deployments, the people who wait for you, the sacrifices made quietly at home. It taught me that even when the battlefield looks the same, you don't. Each return changes you. Each shock—whether from war or from the earth itself—marks you.

By the time I left Gjilane for the last time, I knew I was carrying more than just memories of patrols. I was carrying the weight of love, of responsibility, of a future I wasn't willing to gamble.

Kosovo was where war stopped being an abstract duty and became a test of endurance—of body, of mind, of faith, of family. And though the missions ended, the lessons stayed, shaping every choice I would make in the years to come.

Chapter 6:
Baptized by War — Faith in Fire

It was not long after returning from my second tour in Kosovo, my unit — 2-14 Infantry, part of the 10th Mountain Division — received the order we had been waiting for, and perhaps dreading: prepare to go to war in Iraq. This wasn't another Balkan "peacekeeping" mission, the kind that had been stamped into our passports and our memories for years. This was the real thing — combat. The tone changed immediately. The jokes in the barracks were still there, but they were nervous ones now, laced with a sharp edge. We all understood that this deployment was different. Kosovo had its tense moments, Bosnia even more so, but this was war in every sense of the word. The risks were no longer theoretical. This time, some of us wouldn't be coming home. Preparing at Fort Drum The Army shifted into fast-forward. Medical readiness checks came first — lining up in cold hallways for vaccinations, eye exams, dental work. It was clinical, impersonal, but behind every signature and stamp was the thought: if I don't pass, I might be left behind. None of us wanted that, even if we secretly feared what lay ahead. Then came the paperwork that hit us harder than the needles: wills, powers of attorney, emergency contact updates. Filling out forms that asked who should receive your belongings if you were killed forced each of us to stare the mission square in the face. It was a sobering ritual. I remember sitting at a clerks desk in a cramped office, pen in hand, my wife's name filling line after line. My mind drifted — imagining her alone, imagining futures that might never happen. I signed anyway, because that's what soldiers do. Packing for Iraq felt different too. The familiar rucksacks, rifles, and camouflage were there, but now everything had an added weight, as though the gear itself understood what was coming. Some of the guys added small comforts — a deck of cards, a favorite book, a photo tucked into a helmet liner. These things mattered, talismans against the uncertainty ahead.

The Army shifted into overdrive. Kosovo had long patrols and border checks, Bosnia had been bunkers and wire, but Iraq was going to be another world. Every day was consumed by preparation.

Medical readiness came first. We lined up in cold, echoing hallways like cattle, waiting our turn for shot after shot. Anthrax, smallpox, and boosters for everything in between. The anthrax vaccine burned going in, and the rumor was the side effects could linger for weeks. Smallpox was worse. They jabbed a bifurcated needle into your arm, a series of punctures that left a welt which scabbed, oozed, and itched for days. We were told not to scratch, not to touch, to keep it covered so we didn't spread it to anyone else. It was a mark — both literal and symbolic — of what lay ahead. No one complained out loud, but you could see the unease in the eyes of even the toughest guys. We weren't just training for war; we were being inoculated for it.

Then came the paperwork that hit harder than any needle. Wills, powers of attorney, emergency contact updates. And the big one: SGLI — Servicemembers' Group Life Insurance. The cap was $400,000. For a nineteen- or twenty-year-old soldier, that sounded like a fortune. But filling out that form meant staring at your own death on paper. *If I die, she gets this. If I don't come home, my family gets that..* Signing those forms felt heavier than any ruck I had ever carried.

After the paperwork came the training. Days on the range stretched from dawn to dusk. We ran live-fire exercises until the sound of rifle cracks and machine-gun bursts became a constant in our heads. Convoy operations became our bread and butter — vehicles lined up nose-to-tail, practicing contact drills again and again. "Contact left!" someone would yell, and the whole line had to react: security out, rifles up, suppressing fire, bounding into position, clearing the threat before rolling on. We repeated it until it was muscle memory, because in Iraq hesitation meant death.

Every detail mattered. Weapons were broken down and cleaned until they gleamed, reassembled and checked with almost obsessive care. Radios were tested, re-tested, and then tested again. Trucks were loaded and unloaded, gear tied down, maps traced with fingers in cold barracks rooms. Even the smallest piece of kit was accounted for. If it didn't work perfectly in training, it might kill you in combat.

And then there were the uniforms. For years we had worn woodland camo or the old desert "chocolate chips" pulled from storage for exercises. But now, crates arrived with fresh 3-color DCUs — Desert Camouflage Uniforms. Pulling them on for the first time felt different, heavier somehow. These weren't the fatigues of training rotations or Balkan deployments. These were war uniforms. When you saw yourself in that pale tan and brown pattern, there was no mistaking where you were headed.

The mood in the barracks shifted with every rehearsal, every inspection. Guys still cracked jokes, but the humor was edged, forced, a pressure valve. Between drills, the nervous energy leaked out in small ways — some blasted Metallica on boomboxes, some wrote letters home they never mailed, some just cleaned the same rifle three times in one night. Everyone found a ritual to burn off the same thought: *this is it.*

It wasn't just preparation. It was a ritual. Every round fired, every strap tightened, every fold in a new DCU was part of facing the truth we carried quietly: some of us would not be coming home.

Our first leg out of Fort Drum was a long flight across the Atlantic. The aircraft was packed tight, soldiers squeezed shoulder to shoulder with their gear, knees brushing against rifles. The air smelled of sweat, coffee, and nervous anticipation.

When the wheels touched down in Shannon, Ireland, the captain announced over the intercom that it was March 17th — St. Patrick's Day. We looked around at each other and laughed in disbelief. Most of us had at least a trace of green on us, thanks to the M81 woodland camouflage that seemed suddenly festive. For a fleeting moment, the tension lifted. Soldiers with Irish heritage cracked jokes about "coming home," others grinned at the thought of being on Irish soil, even if it was only for a refuel stop.

We weren't allowed out of a secure area, but just being in Ireland on St. Patrick's Day created a strange kind of memory. The irony wasn't lost on any of us: thousands of miles from home, on the way to a war none of us could predict, and here we were, drinking lukewarm coffee from paper cups while wearing green in the land of shamrocks.

From Ireland, we flew to Romania, where our staging ground turned out to be a cluster of hotels near Constanța on the Black Sea. It was surreal. One moment we were soldiers on edge, bracing for combat; the next, we were in hotel rooms with hot showers, clean sheets, and room service. McDonald's delivered to the lobby. If you had the cash, you could get almost any creature comfort you wanted — pizza, cigarettes, even massages.

The irony of that comfort hit us almost as hard as the reality of what was coming. We were locked down, forbidden to leave the hotel grounds, so the town outside remained out of reach. Through the windows, we could see locals strolling the sidewalks, hear laughter drifting from cafés, the buzz of traffic carrying on as if the world wasn't about to tilt. But for us, Romania might as well have been another version of Fort Drum. The walls held us in, and our minds circled around the desert we knew we were heading toward.

That strange limbo was punctuated by reminders of what lay ahead. Platoon sergeants walked the halls with stacks of U.S. cash — money for "essentials" in a place where nothing was guaranteed. It felt old-school, like something out of Vietnam. Then came the headshots. Each of us stood in front of a plain background, a camera snapping our faces straight on. The photos were to be used if we were captured, killed, or needed to be identified. Nobody said that out loud, but we all knew. Standing still for that camera was harder than running a live-fire range.

Our days were consumed by drills. We practiced stacking on doors, sweeping through buildings, clearing rooms with precision. We rehearsed convoy operations again and again, rifles at the ready, eyes sharp. "Contact left!" someone would shout, and the choreography began, even in hotel parking lots. There was little talk of the beaches or the long history of Constanța. Our focus narrowed to Iraq.

At night, the tension leaked out in strange ways. Some guys played cards in the hotel hallways, the slap of decks echoing off marble walls. Others chain-smoked on balconies overlooking the sea, the orange glow of their cigarettes tracing nervous hands in the dark. Conversations always circled back to Iraq. *Would the locals welcome us? Would we be shot at the minute we landed? Were the rumors about chemical weapons true?* Everyone had heard something, and everyone pretended not to care.

For me, Romania was the first time the anticipation shifted into something heavier. We were comfortable, yes — more comfortable than we had any right to be — but it was a hollow comfort. The massages, the burgers, the televisions in the rooms didn't make us forget what was coming. They only reminded us that the clock was ticking, and when it hit zero, we'd trade sheets for dirt, comfort for chaos, and hotel balconies for rooftops that might hide a rifle barrel.

When the wheels of the C-130 slammed into the runway at Erbil, the silence inside the plane was thicker than the roar of the engines. We had rehearsed this moment in our minds a thousand times: tracer fire streaking the sky, mortars thumping in the distance, chaos waiting at the end of the ramp. But when the tailgate dropped and we shuffled out into the Iraqi night, none of that was there.

The air was heavy with dust and diesel fumes, the kind that coated your tongue and clung to your uniform. Floodlights cast hard beams across the tarmac, throwing long shadows of men and gear, but beyond that pool of light the darkness felt endless. We stacked our rucks in piles, rifles slung across our chests, waiting for something to happen. But nothing did. No explosions, no gunfire, no screaming crowds. Just the hum of generators and the distant night.

It was almost unsettling how quiet it was. After months of preparation, of bracing ourselves for an immediate baptism by fire, we found ourselves lying on the cold concrete, helmets for pillows, staring up at a sky littered with stars. It wasn't fear that kept us awake that night — it was caution. The silence didn't feel safe. It felt like a pause, like the opening page of a story we couldn't yet read.

I remember rolling onto my side, cheek pressed against my NBC mask carrier, listening to the small sounds around me: boots shifting, Velcro ripping, a canteen cap twisting off. Normal noises, soldier noises, but amplified by the stillness. I pulled out my poncho liner — the "woobie." Every infantryman's best friend. Thin, woodland camo, and stitched from nylon and batting, it wasn't much to look at, but it was worth its weight in gold. The woobie was more than a blanket; it was a shield against the cold, a piece of home, a reminder that even in the middle of a combat zone, you could wrap yourself in something familiar.

That night, under a foreign sky in a place we had only seen on maps, I tucked the woobie around my shoulders and let it take the edge off the chill seeping up from the concrete. For a few hours, with my rifle close and body armor still on, it gave me the only comfort a soldier could ask for: enough warmth to close my eyes without shivering.

We weren't afraid yet — but we were guarded. Every shadow looked like it might hold an answer, every light on the horizon a question. That first night in Iraq didn't feel like war. It felt like waiting for war to arrive, wrapped in the thin comfort of a woobie under the desert stars.

The next morning, the stillness broke. We shook the dust from our uniforms, packed our rucks, and were herded toward a line of battered HINO local trucks waiting just off the tarmac. They weren't the armored vehicles we had trained on at Fort Drum — no bulletproof glass, no reinforced plating. Just boxy frames with hard benches and canvas tops, relics that looked like they belonged in another war.

We loaded in, shoulder to shoulder, rifles across our laps, helmets bobbing with every jolt. The road out of Erbil was rough, dust clouds kicking up so thick you could barely see the truck in front of you. The silence of the first night gave way to the grind of gears, the rattle of loose metal, and the occasional cough from soldiers pulling diesel fumes deep into their lungs.

When we finally reached the forward base, the mood shifted again. The Special Forces guys were already there, moving with a quiet confidence that told us they had been living this reality long before we showed up. They didn't waste words, didn't puff their chests. They just looked at us, nodded, and folded us into their rhythm. We respected them immediately.

Our platoon was attached to one of their Alpha detachments, which meant we had a crash course in how to operate their way. Everything was faster, sharper, more deliberate. They moved like chess players who had already seen the board five moves ahead. It rubbed off on us quickly.

But it wasn't just the 10th Group. There were also the Peshmerga.

The first time I saw them roll up, it was like stepping into another world. They weren't polished like U.S. soldiers — no matching uniforms, no standardized gear. Some wore mismatched camouflage, others civilian clothes under chest rigs. Their vehicles were beat-up Land Rovers and Toyotas with rusted frames and bullet holes that hadn't bothered to be patched. And yet, they carried themselves with a kind of confidence that no issued kit could buy. These men had been fighting for their homeland their entire lives.

The Pesh weren't big on formalities. They smoked constantly, laughed loudly, and carried weapons slung casually, like extensions of their own arms. They had scars, missing teeth, eyes that had seen more than most of us could imagine. And when we went on patrol with them, they moved like they owned the ground under their boots. They knew the hills, the villages, the roads that twisted through northern Iraq. Where we relied on maps and GPS, they relied on memory and instinct.

It was humbling, and at times frustrating. They didn't follow U.S. doctrine, didn't clear corners the way we drilled, didn't move in formation the way we practiced at Drum. But they got results. They knew when trouble was brewing, where weapons were stashed, which families were likely to tip off insurgents. Fighting was personal to them in a way it could never be for us.

We learned quickly to balance the two worlds — the discipline and precision of Special Forces, and the gritty, unpolished confidence of the Peshmerga. Somewhere between those extremes, our platoon carved its place.

In less than twenty-four hours, I had gone from lying under the stars with a woobie pulled to my chin to patrolling Iraqi roads alongside men who had been born into conflict. The waiting was over. The mission had begun.

On paper, our missions in Mosul were simple: provide security for the Special Forces teams, back them up when needed, and hold ground so they could do their work. But paper doesn't capture the way your chest tightens when you roll down a narrow alley in a convoy, the way every window seems to hold a set of eyes, the way silence itself feels like an ambush waiting to spring.

The men of 10th Group had been living in that reality for years. You could see it in the way they moved, the way they scanned without seeming to, the way they never wasted a word. They weren't loud or flashy. They carried themselves with a calm that came from surviving situations the rest of us had only trained for. Within days, it was clear: they didn't just tolerate us being there — they folded us in, treating us less like extra muscle and more like teammates. That small gesture of respect meant everything.

The Green Berets taught without ever making it feel like teaching. It was in the details. One showed us how to use the tight corners of Mosul's alleys to set up a hasty ambush, how angles could be more effective than open firepower. Another walked us through how to move inside compounds, teaching us that silence was a weapon — even the clink of gear could give you away if you weren't careful.

They didn't preach. They just demonstrated, then let you absorb it. Their way of soldiering wasn't about volume or bravado; it was about precision and patience. We soaked it up. Even the smallest correction from one of them felt like gold.

It was humbling. In the regular Army, you could hide in the crowd if you wanted to. In their world, you couldn't. Every mistake stood out, and every success mattered. They expected you to raise your game — and you did, because the alternative was being dead weight.

The strangest part was how small the Army world turned out to be. Some of the SF guys were men I had known years earlier in Germany. Back then, we'd been just soldiers on weekends off, chasing beers through cobblestone streets, talking about women and soccer, never imagining where life would take us. Now, we were in northern Iraq, wearing different patches but standing side by side again, this time carrying live rounds instead of hangovers.

War has a way of collapsing time and geography. One day you're leaning on a bar in Baumholder, the next you're leaning against a Land Rover door in Mosul, scanning rooftops for snipers with that same guy you last saw laughing over a pint. The contrast was surreal, but it also grounded us. It was a reminder that life before Iraq was real, that there was a world beyond the dust and checkpoints, and that maybe we'd see it again.

At night, when the city quieted and the radios settled into their static hum, we'd find each other in the glow of the generators and talk about those old days. About Baumholder and wild nights at Kelly's Irish Pub. About the German countryside and the endless beer festivals. We'd laugh about stupid things we'd done as young soldiers, the kind of stories that seemed a lifetime away but still felt like yesterday.

Those conversations were more than nostalgia. They were lifelines. Iraq had a way of making you feel like the whole world had shrunk to the wire around your base. Talking about Germany, about life outside of combat zones, reminded us that the world was still spinning, still waiting for us. It gave us something to hold onto when the only other things around were rifles, dust, and the weight of uncertainty.

In the end, those missions weren't just about guarding Special Forces or patrolling Mosul's streets. They were about becoming sharper, learning from men who had been living this life for decades, and finding pieces of ourselves — and our pasts — in the middle of a war that seemed determined to strip everything else away.

Those weeks in Mosul often felt like we were chasing shadows. The irony was, we were armed to the teeth, loaded down with rifles, grenades, and radios, yet the enemy we had trained so hard to face seemed to vanish into rumor. We rolled through dusty streets, boots crunching gravel, vehicles idling low as we scanned rooftops, alleyways, and every cracked windowpane. The stillness wasn't peace—it was camouflage.

Your body stayed locked on high alert. Muscles tense, eyes burning from hours of scanning. A curtain moved in the breeze and your finger tightened on the trigger. A car slowed at an intersection and your heart pounded, calculating distance, cover, and what would happen if the trunk suddenly popped. Even children playing soccer in the street made you second-guess yourself. Were they just kids chasing a ball, or were they bait, waiting for you to relax so someone else could strike?

That was the cruel part of patrolling ghosts: the uncertainty. A firefight was brutal, but it gave you clarity—an enemy, a direction, a reason to shoot and move. Silence, on the other hand, fed paranoia. Every shadow became a threat, every glance from a bystander an accusation. The quiet was more exhausting than combat.

And yet, we still had our moments of chaos. Short bursts of violence that erupted without warning—rifle cracks echoing off stone walls, the whiplash of returning fire, smoke and dust hanging in the air like a curtain. Then, just as quickly, silence returned, leaving you shaken and wondering if it had even happened. Nothing decisive. Nothing like the pitched battles other units faced in Baghdad or Fallujah. Just flashes, enough to remind you the danger was real, but never enough to release the tension. It felt like patrolling through a pause in history—a storm hovering just out of sight, daring you to blink first.

Some missions were stranger than others. Guarding the radio station, for example. It was a squat compound, surrounded by concrete walls and rusting barbed wire, barely holding itself together. On the surface, it seemed like a pointless task. Guard the airwaves while the city crumbled around it? But those broadcasts mattered. They carried news to locals, orders to civil authorities, and signals to our own units. In a war where rumor spread faster than bullets, keeping a radio tower secure meant keeping a lifeline alive.

Other days we patrolled Mosul University. It was eerie—lecture halls frozen in time, chalk still smeared across boards, books scattered across desks as if students had fled mid-sentence. The echo of boots in those silent corridors made your skin prickle. You could almost hear the ghosts of young voices debating politics, reading poetry, dreaming of futures that had been stolen. Walking through those ruins was a reminder of what war devours first: potential.

And then there was Nineveh. Even saying the name made your tongue pause. This wasn't just a city block or a radio compound—it was one of the oldest inhabited places on earth. The cradle of civilization. Prophets had walked there. Empires had risen and collapsed there. And now, here we were, a platoon of American soldiers, slinging rifles and checking corners, patrolling streets that had already survived thousands of years of blood and fire.

Standing guard with an M4 across my chest in the shadow of ruins older than anything I had ever known, I felt caught between two timelines. The historian in me couldn't ignore the weight of it—the worn stones, the crumbling walls, the whispers of civilizations long gone. And yet, the soldier in me never relaxed, eyes sweeping the horizon, finger brushing the trigger guard, waiting for the danger that might leap out at any moment.

That duality haunted me: standing in history while writing it. Every step we took added another layer to the story of that place. I wondered if, a thousand years from now, anyone would care that a platoon from the 10th Mountain Division once guarded the gates of Nineveh. Or would we, too, be reduced to whispers in the dust?

Back at base, life alternated between crushing monotony and sudden tension. Meals were wolfed down with one hand while the other adjusted a rifle sling. Sleep came in fragments, broken by the whine of vehicles, the crackle of radios, or the sudden order to move out. We slept on a marble floor most nights, poncho liners pulled over us, rifles within reach. Comfort wasn't in mattresses or pillows—it was in the sound of your buddy snoring beside you, a reminder that you weren't alone.

In those slivers of downtime, camaraderie was the only relief. Cigarettes passed hand to hand in the dark. Jokes traded across the room until laughter drowned out, for a moment, the low hum of tension. Even a pair of worn cards became treasure. Those little rituals were how we stayed human when everything else tried to strip humanity away.

The Special Forces guys added their own layer of calm. They had been through more than we could imagine, yet they never carried themselves with bravado. When they spoke, it was measured, deliberate—lessons drawn from Afghanistan, Africa, and wars we hadn't even heard about. We leaned in when they talked, soaking up their hard-won wisdom like students at the feet of professors. They never needed to remind us of their experience; it radiated off them.

It was in that strange rhythm—patrolling ghosts by day, guarding ruins by night, listening to quiet professionals in the dim glow of a generator—that Mosul imprinted itself on me. Not as a place of constant battle, but as a place of waiting, of tension, of learning to live in the silence between gunshots.

Through it all, the thought of home never left me. No matter how many patrols I went on, no matter how many times I scanned rooftops or checked alleyways, a part of my mind was always thousands of miles away—in New York, with my wife. She was pregnant with our first child, a son.

Communication was rare and precious. Phone calls came only when the lines were open, and even then they were short, expensive, and full of static. You learned to condense whole worlds into two or three minutes. "I'm okay." "I miss you." "I love you." Every word had to carry more weight than the sentence itself. When the line clicked off, you were left replaying her voice in your head, holding onto it like a lifeline.

At night, lying under desert stars, poncho liner pulled up against the chill, I tried to picture her belly growing as the months ticked by. I imagined her restless sleep, her discomfort, and her quiet anticipation. I saw her hand resting where our child kicked. The contrast was almost unbearable—life blooming there while death lurked here.

It gnawed at me that I wasn't there. I wasn't the one holding her hand through the long nights, the doctor visits, the uncertainty. She was facing her battle alone, while I was living another kind of battle in Iraq. That guilt became its own kind of weight—one I carried alongside body armor and ammunition.

And then, the unexpected happened. The higher-ups announced that things in Mosul were "stable enough" that a handful of us could rotate home briefly for critical family events. It was rare, almost unheard of. When I heard my name, I didn't believe it at first. The request was approved: I would go home for the birth of my son.

The transition was pure whiplash. One day I was in Iraq, dust caked into my boots, rifle slung across my chest, rehearsing battle drills with Special Forces. The next, I was on a flight, watching the desert fade into clouds, my mind struggling to catch up with the shift. Less than twenty-four hours after leaving a combat zone, I was back in New York.

The hospital was its own kind of battlefield. The fluorescent lights hummed overhead, the air smelled of antiseptic and coffee, and the urgency in the room carried the same intensity as a combat operation. My wife was in labor, exhausted but fierce, fighting her own fight. Nurses moved quickly, doctors issued clipped orders, machines beeped like radios in the field.

I felt helpless in a way combat had never made me feel. In Iraq, I carried a weapon, I had training, I knew what to do when the shooting started. In that hospital room, I was unarmed, untrained, just a man trying to hold his wife's hand and whisper strength into her ear while fear gripped me harder than it ever had under fire.

The delivery turned urgent—an emergency C-section. My chest tightened with a fear I hadn't known, not even on patrols where every alley might conceal an ambush. And then, in what felt like the blink of an eye, he was there. My son. Tiny, fragile, swaddled in blankets, his cries sharper than any gunshot.

I held him in my arms, the weight of him impossibly light yet crushing with significance. Less than forty-eight hours earlier, I had been standing in Nineveh, rifle at the ready, patrolling ruins older than anything I had ever touched. Now, I was cradling a new life—my life, our life—in a hospital room back home.

It was the most profound shift I had ever experienced. From scanning rooftops for snipers to counting tiny fingers and toes. From the dust and diesel fumes of Iraq to the sterile hum of machines in maternity. From war to fatherhood in under two days.

That moment marked me forever. It taught me that life isn't one straight line—it's many stories running in parallel, sometimes colliding in ways you could never plan for. While ancient stones in Nineveh bore silent witness to empires that had risen and fallen, I was beginning my own chapter as a father. While wars burned in foreign lands, a new life began in a hospital room back home.

For the first time, I understood that service wasn't just about carrying a rifle or guarding a checkpoint. It was also about carrying the weight of family, of love, of futures that depended on you making it home. My son's first cry was a reminder that the stakes of war weren't just measured in missions completed or ground secured. They were measured in moments like this—moments worth surviving for.

Chapter 7:
Return to Iraq — Scars Reopened

In between my first and second tours in Iraq, I learned that not all casualties of war wear uniforms or fall on battlefields. My first marriage cracked under the weight of distance, deployments, and the slow erosion of intimacy that comes when months apart stretch into years. By the time I returned home from Iraq 1.0, the damage was done. There were no firefights in our kitchen, no IEDs in our living room, but the war had done its work just the same. My first marriage became another casualty of a conflict thousands of miles away.

I remarried, carrying both scars and hope into that new chapter. My new wife and I built something fragile but beautiful. She was expecting our daughter when the word came down that Iraq was looming again. We had done this dance before — the medical checks, the wills, the paperwork, the gear layouts — but this time it felt heavier. We all knew Iraq 2.0 would be a completely different animal.

If Iraq the first time was like a pit bull on a leash in your neighborhood—contained but still dangerous—then Iraq the second time was a pack of twenty pit bulls, starved for days and let loose in a butcher shop. The leash was gone. The rage was loose. And we were about to walk right into it.

My unit deployed without me. It was a strange mercy. I had been granted leave to stay behind for the birth of my daughter. My new best friend, Henry, deployed with the others. We'd grown close, the kind of friendship that only forms in the spaces between danger and downtime. He had a quick wit, a stubborn streak, and a loyalty that reminded me why brothers-in-arms are different from friends back home. When his wife Emily came around, she became like family too.

As I held my wife's hand, waiting for our daughter's arrival, I couldn't shake the guilt that my brothers were already in Baghdad while I was safe in New York. I told myself it was temporary. Soon I would join them. Soon I would carry my share of the burden.

But war doesn't wait for anyone.

On August 17, 2004, the call came. One of the soldiers in my platoon, a friend named Brandon Titus, had been killed by an explosive device.

The news rippled through the rear detachment like a shockwave. We were thousands of miles from Baghdad, but at that moment, the war arrived in New York. It was no longer something happening "over there." It was here, in our ranks, in our hearts.

The next 24 hours were a blur. Those of us left behind began preparing for funeral duty. Uniforms had to be pressed until there wasn't a wrinkle, boots shined until they reflected light, every movement rehearsed with absolute precision. There is no room for mistakes when you are honoring the dead. The Army drills it into you that the funeral is the last gift you can give a fallen brother.

As I pinned my medals and straightened my uniform, it hit me in a way the battlefield never had: Brandon was gone. Not just deployed. Not just wounded. Gone. And now, instead of preparing for war, I was preparing to fold a flag.

The next day, August 18, 2004, the phone rang at our company's orderly desk. I answered, and on the other end was Emily, Henry's wife. Her voice was ragged with panic, broken by sobs.

Through the tears she explained: she had been out shopping, and when she came home, one of her neighbors told her that two men in uniform had been at her door looking for her. Every military wife knows what that means. And it's never good news.

I tried to steady my voice, to keep it calm for her. "Emily, just stay home," I told her. "I'll find out what's going on."

The truth was, I didn't know anything. My stomach churned as I hung up the phone. I contacted the head of the rear detachment, hoping he could give me something solid. He couldn't confirm or deny, not yet. But he asked me, "Is Emily at home?"

"Yes," I said.

"Good. Keep her there."

He left, and when he came back, I could read the answer on his face even before he said a word. He had spoken to the higher-ups. The official process was in motion.

He knew how close Henry and I were. He put a hand on my shoulder and said quietly, "You should probably go get your wife and go to Emily's house."

And that's when the truth came down like a hammer. Henry had been shot. And he was gone.

Within 24 hours, I had lost a good friend and my best friend.

While the company prepared Brandon's funeral, Emily made a request that humbled me: she wanted me to escort Henry home from Dover Air Force Base to Colorado.

I won't go into every detail. Some moments are too sacred, too raw, to lay bare. But I will say this: up until that point in my life, it was the hardest thing I had ever done.

The flight from Dover carried not just Henry's body but the weight of everything we had shared — the laughs, the plans, the bond that only comes from soldiering together. Sitting in that aircraft, thinking about the flag-draped coffin, I felt the war in my bones in a way no firefight ever had.

In Colorado, I walked with his family, stood by Emily, and tried to be strong while my insides felt hollowed out. I had no script, no manual. Just grief and the duty to bear it well.

I was fortunate, though. A senior NCO, Gene. He guided me, mentored me, and taught me how to carry the unbearable weight of escort duty. His words and steady presence were a lifeline. I'll never forget that. Thank you, Gene.

Henry's funeral was still fresh in my heart when I boarded a plane to Iraq. The timing was merciless. There was no chance to heal, no space to grieve properly. My daughter had just been born. My best friend had just been buried. And now I was being pulled back into the maw of war.

When I arrived, I joined my platoon, a platoon that had already lost two and suffered multiple wounds in a very short span. The men I rejoined weren't the same ones who had left Fort Drum. Their eyes were harder, their voices quieter, their movements sharper with the edge of men who had already paid in blood.

This time, Iraq was different. This time, we were headed into the heart of hell.

I could feel the difference immediately. These weren't the same men who had left Fort Drum with me months earlier. They carried themselves differently now — their shoulders a little lower, their eyes a little harder, their conversations shorter and sharper. Grief had left its mark on them, and so had combat.

I had missed the opening act of Iraq 2.0, but the second act had no intermission. The moment my boots hit the dust of Baghdad, I knew the leash was off. This wasn't northern Iraq, where we patrolled ghost neighborhoods and fired only sporadically. This was Sadr City.

Sadr City sat in eastern Baghdad, a dense, sprawling slum that felt like a city within a city. It was home to millions, most of them Shi'a, many loyal to Muqtada al-Sadr, a radical cleric with deep ties to Iran. His Mahdi Army controlled much of the ground, and we knew from day one we weren't welcome.

The streets were tight, claustrophobic, lined with cinderblock buildings pockmarked from old battles. Vendors sold vegetables, meat, and scraps under corrugated tin roofs. Children played in the streets, sometimes waving, sometimes glaring, sometimes gathering in ways that made you wonder if they were spotters for insurgents. Above it all, a tangle of power lines sagged like spiderwebs, a mess of black cables that always made me wonder which ones were actually transmitting electricity and which ones were just waiting to spark a fire.

Driving into Sadr City felt like walking into the jaws of a beast. You never knew which block would explode, which corner would spit out gunfire. Every alley had the potential to hide an RPG team, every pile of trash might conceal an IED.

Our patrols became a grind. We'd mount up, roll out in Humvees, and snake our way through the streets. The routine never felt routine. Every turn of the wheel could be the last.

IEDs were constant. Some were crude — artillery shells buried in the dirt with det cord snaking back to a trigger man. Others were sophisticated, pressure plates hidden under trash or shaped charges waiting to gut a vehicle. The boom of an IED was something you never got used to. It started with a flash, a sound that rattled your bones, and then the chaos of dust, smoke, and screaming over radios.

RPGs came next, streaks of fire lancing out of alleys. Sometimes they missed, sometimes they hit. We learned to spot the telltale signs — a sudden clearing of people from a street, a door closing just as you drove past. But often, there was no warning. Just impact.

Small arms fire was a given. Pop shots from rooftops, bursts from AK-47s. Sometimes we could return fire, sometimes the shooters melted away into the city before we could pin them down.

The stress wasn't just physical, it was mental. Every patrol was a test of nerves. You learned to watch the children's eyes, the rhythm of foot traffic, the sound of the city. Sadr City spoke a language, and you had to learn it quickly to survive.

The Weight of Loss

The casualties piled up quickly. Names etched themselves into our memories, each one a brother gone.

Glenn Allison

Brandon Titus

Henry Risner

David Waters

Brian Baker

Dwayne McFarlane

Lindsey James

Darren Deblanc

Charles Cooper

Kurt Schamberg

John Klinesmith

Jason Denfrund*

Shawn Clemens*

Travis Atkins* - Medal Of Honor Recipient

Each name carried a face, a laugh, a memory. They weren't just soldiers. They were part of us. And with each loss, the unit grew smaller, the burden heavier.

* Clemens was killed in Afghanistan 2004

*Denfrund and Atkins both in Iraq 3.0

Sadr City had a rhythm all its own. Mornings often began with explosions — a patrol from another unit hit by an IED, the sound echoing across the district. Midday brought the crack of sniper fire or the sudden rush of a firefight. By evening, we were usually exhausted, bodies sore, nerves raw.

Sleep came in fits, broken by indirect fire, mortars dropping into the base like angry fists from the sky. You'd wake up with your heart pounding, dust in your mouth, listening for the next impact.

In between, we lived in fragments. Letters from home. Cigarettes smoked down to the filter. Jokes told in Humvees to cover the silence. We trained ourselves to be alert and numb at the same time — a paradox that kept us alive.

Unlike Iraq 1.0, where locals sometimes waved and kids chased after us, Sadr City was a different world. Here, we were occupiers, targets, intruders. You could feel the hostility in the way eyes followed you, the way conversations stopped when you entered a market.

Sometimes children threw rocks at our vehicles. Sometimes they just stared with expressions far too old for their young faces. You never knew which teenager might be holding a cell phone to trigger an IED, which shopkeeper might be hiding rifles in the back. The lines between civilian and combatant blurred until everyone felt like a potential enemy.

It wore on you. It hardened you. And it left scars you couldn't see until years later.

For me, every patrol carried a ghost. Henry was with me in every street, every alley, every rooftop scan. His absence was a constant presence. I thought about the conversations we never finished, the beers we never drank, the stories we never got to tell.

Sometimes I imagined what he would say about the madness of Sadr City, about the chaos that had swallowed us whole. Other times, I imagined him walking beside me, steady and calm, the way he always was. Carrying his memory kept me moving forward, even when the weight felt unbearable.

Iraq 2.0 was nothing like Iraq 1.0. The leash was gone, the chaos unbound. It wasn't about securing airports or patrolling historic ruins. It was about surviving day to day in a city that wanted us dead.

I carried the loss of my brothers, the weight of my daughter's birth, and the constant edge of combat. It was a crucible that burned away illusions and left only the raw truth: war is not about glory. It is about endurance, sacrifice, and loss.

We fought, we bled, and we survived — some of us. The names of the fallen remain etched in my heart, a roll call I will never forget.

Chapter 8:

A Zionist Awakens — Convictions Forged

I guess you could say my understanding of justice and injustice—especially when it came to ethnic and religious conflict—was forged long before I ever heard the word *Zionism*. It didn't arrive in my life as a lightning bolt or some grand conversion moment. It was more like a series of hammer blows—each one shaping me a little more, each one driving home a truth I couldn't ignore.

The first blow came in childhood, in a Massachusetts classroom, where I learned about the Holocaust. The word itself carried weight I didn't yet understand, but the images, the testimony, the numbers burned into a survivor's arm—they forced me to confront what hate could do when left unchecked. It was no longer abstract history. It was humanity at its worst, seared into memory.

Years later, the lessons of those classrooms were no longer confined to books or films. They took flesh before my eyes when I deployed as a soldier. Bosnia. Kosovo. Iraq. Places where hatred wasn't an academic subject or a documentary reel—it was present, alive, and bleeding. I stood among ruins where neighbors had butchered neighbors because of faith, language, or bloodline. I guarded roads littered with mass graves. I saw mothers bury children while politicians debated resolutions oceans away.

Each encounter was another reminder: hatred doesn't dissolve with time. It doesn't evaporate into memory. When unchecked, it festers. It passes from fathers to sons, from preachers to congregations, from textbooks to classrooms. Left alone, it grows.

And the other truth was just as brutal: without a homeland, without power to defend themselves, vulnerable people rarely survive. History proved it in Europe's ghettos and death camps. I saw it echoed in the Balkans. I watched it repeat itself in the streets of Iraq. The world might mourn after the fact, but rarely does it step in before the killing begins.

Zionism wasn't in my vocabulary yet. But the soil it grows from—this recognition of the human need for safety, sovereignty, and survival—was already planted deep inside me.

In public school, Holocaust education wasn't just another subject. It was a reckoning. By the time the curriculum reached the Holocaust, I was already fascinated—maybe even fixated—on World War II. While other kids were reading sports magazines or comic books, I was poring over histories of D-Day, the Battle of the Bulge, Stalingrad. The maps, the strategy, the sheer scale of destruction drew me in. Europe during the 1940s became a kind of obsession.

But the military campaigns, as dramatic as they were, always carried shadows. For every story of paratroopers dropping behind enemy lines, there was another about a Jewish family rounded up in a cattle car. The deeper I dug into the war, the harder it was to ignore that the Holocaust wasn't a footnote to the fighting—it was its own central story. The battles liberated camps. The flags raised over Berlin didn't just end the war; they pulled back the curtain on humanity's darkest chapter.

That obsession came into sharper focus the day a survivor spoke in our school auditorium. He was a small man, his voice quiet, but when he rolled up his sleeve and showed us the numbers tattooed into his arm, the room fell silent in a way I had never experienced. Those numbers weren't abstract. They weren't statistics in a textbook. They were the mark of attempted erasure, etched into living flesh. For me, it was like one of the history books I had devoured suddenly reached out and grabbed me by the collar.

We read *Night* by Elie Wiesel soon after, and I wrestled with sentences that haunted me for weeks. They weren't just words—they were reminders that while Patton's tanks rolled east and Eisenhower planned his invasions, there were people starving in ghettos, being herded into gas chambers, stripped not just of life but of dignity. Watching *Schindler's List* later on only deepened that sense. The black-and-white images of Jews clutching their mothers' skirts, trains bound for Auschwitz, guards barking orders—it didn't feel like a Hollywood film to me. It felt like another chapter in the military histories I had been devouring, only this time the "front line" was inside the wire of barbed fences.

Teachers spoke of the six million, but it was the individual stories that sank deepest into me: a violinist who never played again, a family that vanished save for one child, a rabbi who continued to pray even in the camps. What struck me most wasn't just the cruelty of the Nazis, but the complicity of the world. How so many people—neighbors, officials, entire nations—stood by or turned away. The same countries whose generals I studied with admiration had leaders who, for too long, ignored the cries of the doomed.

The refrain of "Never Again" echoed through those lessons. But even then, with my head full of battles and maps, I felt a nagging suspicion: humanity doesn't learn lessons easily. Wars end, but the hatred that fuels them lingers. And if it happened once, it could happen again.

That suspicion—that hatred never really dies, it just waits—was confirmed when I found myself in the Balkans in the late 1990s. Twice in

Bosnia, twice in Kosovo. By the time I arrived, the wars were technically "over," at least on paper. Treaties had been signed, international forces deployed. But walking those streets, you could feel it: the conflict wasn't over. It was smoldering just below the surface, its shadows stretching across every village, every face.

The land itself bore scars that looked permanent. Burned-out houses dotted the countryside like tombstones, their roofs collapsed, walls riddled with bullet holes. Churches stood desecrated, their altars smashed. Mosques were blown apart, minarets toppled. Cemeteries had been vandalized—headstones cracked, inscriptions defaced, graves ripped open. It wasn't just war; it was erasure. A deliberate attempt to destroy not only people but memory, heritage, continuity.

And then there were the graves. Mass graves unearthed by international teams, skeletons stacked like cordwood, blindfolds still tied, hands bound behind backs. I had seen pictures of such things in history books, black-and-white photographs from Poland and Germany. Now, standing on Balkan soil, I saw the same thing with my own eyes. Different uniforms, different languages, different victims. But the same hatred. The same intent.

The Serbs targeted Bosniaks and Kosovars because of their identity—Muslim, Albanian, "other." Just as the Nazis had targeted Jews, Roma, homosexuals, and anyone who did not fit the twisted ideal of "purity." It wasn't about resources, or land, or even politics, though those played their roles. At its core, it was about identity, and the decision that certain identities did not deserve to live. I walked streets where neighbors had slaughtered neighbors, not over money or fences, but over ancestry. That was what made it feel so chillingly familiar.

The parallels were undeniable. I remembered sitting in a classroom in Brookline, reading Elie Wiesel's *Night*, staring at the black-and-white photos of skeletal figures behind barbed wire, hearing a Holocaust survivor describe being treated as less than human. And now, in the 1990s, half a world away, I was seeing the same patterns repeated. "Never Again" had become "Once Again."

And, just like in the 1940s, the world had hesitated. Bureaucrats in New York and Brussels debated resolutions while villages burned, while women were raped, while the graves filled. By the time NATO intervened with force, entire communities had already been erased. It was as if the world had learned nothing from the camps and the crematoria.

One evening, I stood in a town square, children swarming us in hopes of candy or soccer balls. Behind them loomed a row of shops, half-collapsed from shelling. Their laughter clashed with the ruins, a haunting dissonance. As the kids tugged at our sleeves, an old man watched from a doorway. His face was carved with grief, eyes hollow, like someone who had seen more funerals than birthdays.

At that moment, I thought of the man who had spoken in my school years before, the survivor who had shown us the numbers tattooed on his arm. The look in the old man's eyes was the same: a witness to hatred at its ugliest. Different continents. Different century. Different victims. But the same story. Hatred left unchecked doesn't fade—it becomes a firestorm.

Years later, in Iraq, the lessons of Bosnia and Kosovo came back to me with brutal clarity. By then, I already carried the images of mass graves, burned-out villages, and neighbors turning on neighbors. I thought I had seen the depths of what hatred could do. Iraq taught me I was wrong—there were still deeper circles of hell.

My first deployment had been strangely quiet—sporadic firefights, raids with Special Forces, tense but survivable. There were tense patrols through Mosul, brushes with danger, the weight of anticipation. But Iraq 2.0 was different. It was chaos unchained. The country was ripping itself apart at the seams, and we were dropped into the middle of it.

We lost men within weeks. Brandon Titus. My best friend, Henry Risner. Others wounded, scarred, broken. One day we'd share smokes and jokes in the motor pool, the next their absence was a hole you couldn't fill. The funerals still haunt me. Standing in dress uniform, saluting caskets draped in flags, presenting folded triangles of cloth to mothers, wives, children. The sound of taps echoing across cemeteries in Colorado was every bit as haunting as the explosions in Baghdad. Escorting Henry's body back to Colorado was the hardest thing I had ever done. Walking into his hometown, seeing his parents' faces, felt like bringing the war straight into their living room. The Holocaust echo was impossible to miss—families shattered, chairs left empty at dinner tables forever.

Sadr City made the parallels even sharper. It was Bosnia all over again, only louder, hotter, and more crowded. Militias ruled with sectarian fury, Sunnis and Shias tearing at each other with a vengeance as old as their history, driven by clerics who wielded scripture like weapons. Every wall was painted with slogans, every alley whispered of violence. IEDs didn't just target Humvees—they ripped through markets, mosques, and schools. They weren't designed to just kill soldiers, but to kill *hope*.

Children bore the scars. Some limped from shrapnel wounds that would never fully heal. Others had the hollow eyes of those who had seen their parents killed. Some still played soccer in the dust, but even their laughter felt subdued, edged with something darker. In Bosnia, the children begged us for candy. In Iraq, too often, they begged us for protection.

Every patrol felt like moving through a neighborhood where life had been stolen by ideology. Houses stood, people survived, but the spirit was gutted. Sectarian identity was now a death sentence depending on which block you lived on. It was the same logic I had seen in the Balkans—kill or expel because of who someone was, not what they had done. Different language, different faith, same poison.

And once again, I saw the apathy of the world. Politicians in Washington argued about strategies and exit plans. Diplomats drafted resolutions that never left conference rooms. Commentators filled airwaves with debates about oil, insurgency, and policy. Meanwhile, ordinary Iraqis buried their dead. Just as the world had turned its back on Jews in Europe, just as the UN had hesitated while Bosnia burned, so too did leaders wring their hands while Baghdad bled.

The Holocaust. The Balkans. Iraq. To me, they weren't separate conflicts—they were chapters in the same book. A book that taught me one brutal lesson: vulnerable people cannot count on others to save them. They need power, protection, and the will to defend themselves. Otherwise, history repeats itself with different uniforms, different victims, the same graves.

By the time I encountered Zionism as a philosophy—through Herzl's writings, through conversations with Jewish friends and Israeli soldiers—I didn't need convincing of its necessity. I had already seen what happens when people are targeted simply for being who they are. I had already buried brothers who died in wars fueled by ethnic and religious hatred.

Herzl didn't invent Jewish suffering; he simply saw its inevitability in a world where Jews had no state of their own. His call for a homeland wasn't abstract. It was survival. And when I connected his words to what I had seen—in textbooks, in the Balkans, in Baghdad—the picture was clear. Zionism wasn't just an idea. It was justice. It was life.

I first encountered the word Zionism in a serious way sometime after my Balkan deployments. I'd heard it before, of course—thrown around in headlines or political debates, often distorted by those who didn't understand it. But it wasn't until I picked up the writings of Theodor Herzl that I realized it was more than a slogan—it was a lifeline.

Herzl wasn't a prophet in the biblical sense, and he wasn't pretending to be a rabbi. He was a journalist, a thinker, a man who had stared directly at Europe's sickness of antisemitism even in supposedly enlightened, modern societies. His conclusion was simple, radical, and, to me, undeniable: Jews needed sovereignty, not sympathy. They needed a homeland, not hand-wringing.

Reading Herzl after Bosnia and Iraq felt like reading someone who had walked the same ruined streets I had, only decades earlier. He understood the brutal cycle I had already witnessed with my own eyes: people without power become victims, victims become refugees, and the world issues statements while the graves fill. Herzl saw it in Vienna and Paris; I saw it in Srebrenica, in Gjilane, in Sadr City.

For me, his words weren't just political theory. They were prophecies fulfilled—not in distant history books, but in the headlines of my own life.

My understanding of Zionism deepened in Germany, of all places—a country whose soil was still heavy with the memory of Jewish suffering, where the ghosts of the Holocaust lingered in stone memorials and unspoken history lessons. I was stationed there with the U.S. Army when I became close with a fellow soldier who had served in the Israel Defense Forces before joining our ranks.

We spent long nights talking, sometimes over beers in smoky German pubs, sometimes on guard duty with rifles slung across our chests, sometimes in the quiet lulls between drills. His perspective was unlike anything I had ever encountered. For me, war had been something I had trained for and then walked into as an adult. For him, survival wasn't a choice or a job—it was the background music of his entire childhood.

He told me about rocket drills in grade school, how teachers would usher students into shelters with the efficiency of fire drills in America. Except for him, it wasn't hypothetical. The sirens were real, the rockets were real, and the possibility of not making it home from school wasn't something whispered—it was something lived.

He spoke of buses exploding, of friends gone in an instant to suicide bombers. He told me how his parents drilled into him the habit of scanning for exits in every restaurant, every mall, every public place. "Always know your way out," they had told him, the way my parents had once told me to look both ways before crossing the street. It was survival passed down like tradition.

And then he laughed—not cruelly, but at the bitter irony—when he said, "What you saw on tv, I saw at fifteen on my way to school."

What struck me most wasn't just the danger he described—it was the resilience in his stories. He told me about going to the beach in Tel Aviv the day after a bombing, because to stay home would mean letting fear win. He described Friday nights at home, Shabbat candles lit, songs sung, bread broken, laughter echoing even with sirens in the background. Life went on—not in defiance of the danger, but because of it.

For him, Zionism wasn't an ideology to be debated in classrooms or on op-ed pages. It wasn't a question of "left" or "right." It was a birthright, a shield, a reason to keep building even when enemies tried to destroy. It was the very air he breathed, the compass that kept his people alive.

Our conversations weren't always easy. Sometimes we argued, circling over Israel's politics, over its mistakes, over its complicated place in the world. He didn't sugarcoat any of it. He admitted the flaws, the challenges, the constant state of vigilance that wore on people. But every time, his clarity broke through: without Israel, Jews had nowhere to run. Without Israel, "Never Again" was just a slogan waiting to be broken.

And as I listened—whether sitting in a guard tower under a German moon, or hunched over a beer in Kelly's Pub downtown—I realized something simple but profound: for him, Zionism wasn't history. It wasn't a theory. It was home. And in a world where "Never Again" too often becomes "Once More," that home was not negotiable.

By then, I was already convinced. But the more I studied, the more the historical weight of Zionism became impossible to ignore.

The land of Israel wasn't an accident, nor was it a colonial experiment, as so many critics like to claim. It was the ancestral homeland of the Jewish people—attested to by scripture, by archaeology, by the records of empire after empire that once marched across the hills of Judea and Galilee. The stories of the twelve tribes, the united kingdom under David, the Temple in Jerusalem—all of these weren't myths whispered in the dark. They were tangible, rooted in history and stone. You can stand at the Western Wall and touch the same blocks of limestone that Jews prayed toward for centuries. You can walk through ruins in the Galilee where synagogues stood nearly two thousand years ago. The connection wasn't theoretical. It was physical, historical, undeniable.

And history bore this out. Invaders came and went—the Babylonians, Persians, Greeks, Romans, Byzantines, Ottomans, British. Each of them left their mark, chiseling names into walls, stamping coins, building fortresses. But none of them carried the land in their soul the way the Jews did. None of them prayed three times a day toward Jerusalem. None of them broke bread with words of longing for Zion on their lips. None of them ended every Passover Seder with the vow: *"Next year in Jerusalem."*

Even in exile, Jews carried that bond across continents and centuries. In medieval Spain, as the Inquisition bore down, Jews sang psalms yearning for return. In Poland's shtetls, they told their children bedtime stories about Jerusalem as if it were just beyond the next hill. In Baghdad, Yemen,

Morocco—everywhere Jews lived scattered—they planted their hearts in Zion. No other people has sustained such an unbroken connection to one piece of land for millennia. That matters. It is not a coincidence. It is identity.

So when 1948 came, and the State of Israel was declared, it wasn't the birth of something new. It wasn't a colonial outpost carved by foreign powers. It was the return of something ancient, a restoration of dignity after centuries of wandering and persecution. For a people who had carried memory like a burden and a torch, it was the fulfillment of a promise whispered across thousands of years.

Israel's founding was not just political—it was spiritual. It was an answer to exile, a refuge after pogroms, a homecoming after the Holocaust. It was the embodiment of that eternal refrain: *Never Again.*

Zionism, to me, isn't about supremacy. It's about sovereignty. It is about the right of the Jewish people—after centuries of wandering, persecution, and genocide—to live safely and freely in their ancestral homeland. Sovereignty is not arrogance; it is dignity. It is the difference between pleading for protection and being able to guarantee it yourself.

But Zionism has never been about Jews alone. The vision carried forward since Herzl and Ben-Gurion was not of an ethnocracy, but of a nation where others—Christians, Muslims, Druze, Baháʼís—could flourish alongside Jews. That vision, however imperfectly realized, is still visible on the ground.

Israel's enemies point to its flaws, and there are flaws—real ones, the kind any democracy wrestles with. But I've seen the truth up close. I've seen Arab police officers wearing the Star of David on their uniform with pride, not as a mark of subjugation but as a declaration that they serve and belong. I've watched Muslim and Jewish women stand shoulder to shoulder in a shop, laughing together while choosing scarves, an ordinary act that quietly defies every headline shouting "apartheid." I've seen Ethiopian Jews march in IDF parades, Druze officers commanding soldiers, Christian nurses tending to patients without a thought to religion or ethnicity. These weren't staged photo ops. They were daily life.

What makes Zionism remarkable today is that it continues to stand as an island of democracy in a region drowning in dictatorship. Across the Middle East, you find authoritarian regimes, clerical rule, and crushing repression. In Israel, you find vigorous debate, protests in the streets, parties rising and falling through elections, a press free enough to criticize the very leaders it protects. Zionism created not just a state, but a society where freedom is fought for openly.

Modern Zionism is not only about survival. It is about life—about building and creating even under fire. It is about fields in the Negev blooming with agriculture where deserts once stood barren. It is about skyscrapers rising in Tel Aviv, start-ups reshaping technology, and Hebrew—once a "dead" language—being spoken in playgrounds and boardrooms alike. It is about defending against rockets while also sending aid teams to Haiti after an earthquake, or to Africa to help with clean water. Zionism is resilience married to generosity.

Above all, Zionism is a love story. A love of land, of people, of heritage. A love strong enough to endure centuries of exile and hatred, pogroms and ghettos, gas chambers and wars. A love that is stubborn, sometimes bruised, but never extinguished. To believe in Zionism today is not to believe in perfection—it is to believe in permanence.

When I think back to Bosnia, to Kosovo, to Iraq, to the Holocaust testimonies of my youth, one lesson repeats itself with brutal clarity: silence is complicity. The world has a long, shameful habit of looking away when hatred rises. Bureaucrats debate, politicians hedge, neighbors whisper. By the time the world acts, the graves are already dug. "Never Again" becomes "Not Our Problem."

As a soldier, I learned that silence doesn't stop violence—strength does. In Bosnia, silence meant Srebrenica. In Iraq, silence meant militias turning neighborhoods into killing fields. On the ground, the truth was simple: the side that hesitated lost, and the ones who waited for others to save them rarely survived. That lesson applies beyond the battlefield. It applies to nations. It applies to people.

Zionism is the antidote to that silence. It is not an abstract philosophy or a debating point for professors. It is a doctrine of survival, a soldier's creed translated into a nation's existence: never again wait for someone else to defend you. Build your own state. Raise your own army. Train your sons and daughters to fight if necessary, so their children may one day know peace.

For me, as a non-Jew who has walked the ruins of genocide and buried friends lost to sectarian violence, supporting Zionism is not political—it's tactical, it's moral, it's essential. In uniform I learned that security isn't granted; it's earned, defended, and maintained every single day. Israel understands this better than most. Its existence is not guaranteed by treaties or UN resolutions but by the men and women who stand guard, by the tanks and jets that say in unmistakable terms: the Jewish people will never again be passive victims.

If that means I get called names, accused of bias, or excluded from polite circles, so be it. I've stood on ridgelines with men who didn't come home, I've seen the faces of children caught in hatred's crossfire, and I've saluted flag-draped coffins. I know the cost of silence. I know the cost of inaction. Neutrality isn't noble; it's surrender dressed up as sophistication.

Zionism, to me, is not just about Israel—it is about standing against that surrender. It is about survival, about justice, about the simple truth that every person has the right to defend its existence. It means recognizing history not as a burden but as a call to arms, a foundation on which to build.

To stand with Zionism is to say clearly, in a world that prefers ambiguity: Israel has a right to exist. Israel has a right to defend itself. And Israel will endure—not because the world finally learns its lesson, but because the Jewish people refuse to entrust their survival to anyone else ever again.

Chapter 9:

The Breaking Point — Shattered but Unbowed

Saturday, October 7, 2023, began the way so many mornings had for me. The air was crisp with that first bite of New England fall, the kind of weather that makes a hot cup of coffee feel almost holy. I shuffled into the kitchen, half awake, brewed a cup, and settled into my living room couch. Steam curled from the mug in my hand as I opened my phone to scan the news.

For years, this had been my ritual. Coffee and headlines. A way to orient myself to the world before the day really began. Normally, it was politics, sports, maybe a story about the economy or a celebrity scandal. Noise, but familiar noise.

That morning, though, the noise was different. The headlines weren't routine. They screamed. They bled. And as I scrolled, the shape of something apocalyptic came into view. Reports out of Israel. *"Massive attack."* *"Rockets fired from Gaza."* *"Fighting underway."* At first, I thought it was another flare-up—something I had seen countless times in the region. Israel had always been under attack, always under rockets, and they had always endured. But within minutes, the story sharpened. This wasn't just rockets. It wasn't just fighting. Something far worse was unfolding in real time.

The numbers climbed like a nightmare. Dozens dead. Then hundreds. Then more. Young people were massacred at a music festival in the desert. Civilians dragged from their homes. Entire families slaughtered in safe rooms that had become tombs.

I felt the breath leave my chest. My stomach clenched as if I'd been punched. I dropped my phone onto the couch, then scrambled for my laptop. Maybe there was more detail, something clearer, something that would tell me this wasn't happening the way it sounded. I pulled up every site I knew—Israeli news outlets, American papers, Telegram channels, X (still new in my vocabulary after decades of calling it Twitter). The information was chaotic, contradictory, but the through-line was unmistakable: Jews were being hunted, murdered, and dragged across the border like trophies.

And then came the videos.

I knew I shouldn't click them. I knew they would be seared into my mind forever. But I couldn't look away. Within minutes I was watching the raw, unfiltered footage that Hamas itself had uploaded—bragging, laughing, documenting their own crimes. Masked gunmen storming through neighborhoods. Young people sprinting across desert fields as paragliders descended from the sky, terrorists spraying bullets into the crowd. Women dragged by the hair, screaming, as men jeered and filmed. Families huddled in safe rooms, executed point-blank. Houses set ablaze with people still inside.

These weren't accidents. They weren't military operations gone wrong. This was deliberate. This was a theater, staged for the world to watch. Terrorists looked into cameras and smiled as they desecrated bodies. They uploaded the footage themselves, proud of what they had done.

I had seen violence before. Bosnia. Kosovo. Iraq. I knew what men were capable of. I had seen mass graves with my own eyes, escorted bodies home under flags, fought through streets where hatred dictated who lived and who died. But this—this was different. This was savagery stripped bare, a hatred so ancient and so deep it carried the stench of genocide.

And just as sickening as the acts themselves was the certainty in my gut that many in the world would rush to excuse them. That protests in Western cities would find a way to spin this slaughter into "resistance." That academics, pundits, even politicians would parse the language until murder sounded like justice. The thought made me nauseous.

Had Hamas struck purely military targets—bases, checkpoints, convoys—the headlines would still have been grim, the losses still painful. But at least it would have been war. Soldiers fight soldiers. Infrastructure gets hit. That's combat. But this wasn't combat. This was a slaughter. Infants, grandmothers, Holocaust survivors—dragged into Gaza as prizes, paraded through the streets. The intentional targeting of the defenseless revealed everything: Hamas wasn't fighting for freedom. They weren't fighting occupation. They were trying to erase Jews. Period.

As I stared at the footage, I felt an old fire ignite inside me. Rage. Not the kind of passing anger you feel at bad politics or everyday injustice, but the bone-deep rage of a soldier who has seen what happens when evil is allowed to run unchecked. My heart pounded like I was back on patrol, adrenaline flooding my system, scanning rooftops and alleyways for threats. My hands literally shook as I thought: *I need to be there.* If there had been a way to board a plane to Tel Aviv that very moment and enlist in the IDF, I would have done it without hesitation. Vest on, rifle in hand, shoulder to shoulder with my Israeli brothers and sisters. I would have gone back into uniform without a second thought.

That morning, I wasn't just reading the news. I was reliving every lesson of Bosnia, every firefight in Iraq, every time I had stood over a friend's grave.

The parallels screamed at me: hatred doesn't die, it metastasizes. And when Jews are the target, the world shrugs until it's too late.

But Israel hadn't asked. There was no call for international brigades, no foreign volunteers flooding in like in Ukraine. Israel, as always, stood alone. And as much as I respected that, it tore at me. Because for the first time since I hung up my uniform, I wanted to put it back on. I wanted to fight again—not for America this time, but for Israel, for the Jewish people, for the idea that "Never Again" should actually mean something.

The rage hasn't left me. I don't think it ever will.

And then came the second wave of horror—this one not from Gaza, but from right here at home.

Even as Israeli bodies were still warm, even as hostages were being dragged through the streets and paraded like trophies, activists in the West were celebrating. Not condemning. Not grieving. Celebrating.

On campuses across America, student groups rushed out statements of "solidarity with the Palestinian resistance." Resistance? I had just watched raw footage of women raped and murdered on camera. I had seen children executed in their beds. I had seen civilians shot down like animals while fleeing across open fields. And these elite students—the supposed future lawyers, politicians, journalists, the ones who would one day sit in Congress or anchor our news broadcasts—were calling that barbarity "resistance."

In major cities, murals appeared overnight, glorifying paragliders—the very method Hamas terrorists had used to swoop down upon and massacre young festival-goers in the desert. Crowds gathered in the streets, waving flags, chanting: *"From the river to the sea." "Intifada now."* They weren't mourning Jewish dead; they were exalting their killers.

I scrolled in disbelief. Professors, the very people entrusted with shaping young minds, excusing the violence or draping it in the language of "decolonization." Politicians hedging, mumbling about "both sides." Media outlets published headlines that erased the killers and, in subtle but unmistakable ways, blamed the victims.

The mask had slipped. No—scratch that. The mask had been ripped off entirely. The antisemitism that had long simmered beneath polite society, dressed up as "human rights" rhetoric or cloaked in academic jargon, was now naked, proud, and unapologetic. And the worst part? It wasn't just radicals waving signs in faraway corners. It was here, in America. In our universities. In our newsrooms. In the institutions that shape policy, culture, and the future of our nation.

In the days that followed, Israel did what any sovereign nation must do. They mobilized the IDF. They struck back at Hamas. They hunted the perpetrators, launched operations into Gaza, targeted leaders, and tried to rescue hostages. They did what every government owes its citizens: defend them.

And yet, the global protests didn't erupt against Hamas. They erupted against Israel. Against the victims. Against the one Jewish state in the world, reeling from the worst massacre of Jews since the Holocaust.

Students staged sit-ins and blocked bridges. Protesters shut down highways and airports. Headlines painted Israel as the aggressor. Politicians called for "restraint," as if restraint were possible when babies were still being held in cages, when women were still hostages in tunnels, when entire families had been wiped off the face of the earth.

The world had turned upside down. Truth collapsed into false equivalence. Decency was swallowed by ideology. It was as if a massive hole had opened in the moral fabric of society, a black hole that sucked in everything—justice, compassion, clarity—and left only rage, lies, and applause for evil.

And in that void, one conviction crystallized in me: someone had to speak. Someone had to stand.

The days after October 7 were a blur, but not the kind of blur that numbs you. This one sharpened me like a blade on stone. Every headline, every video clip, every smug post online excusing slaughter cut into me like glass. I couldn't unsee it, couldn't ignore it, couldn't swallow it down. It became impossible to sit still.

Scrolling through feeds wasn't enough. Venting in conversations with friends wasn't enough. Even donating money to organizations helping victims in Israel felt inadequate. I had been a soldier once. I had walked the ruins of Bosnia, Kosovo, and Iraq. I had seen what hatred does when the world looks away. And now, I was sitting in Massachusetts, watching history repeat itself—watching the Jewish people stand alone again while my own country's elites vilified them.

The urgency burned inside me. It wasn't optional anymore. It was a calling.

It was December when the moment came, though in truth it had been building since that morning in October when the world split in two. I was sitting on my couch, idly clicking through one of the Israel advocacy groups I had joined on Facebook. Most of what I saw was familiar by then—articles I had already read, op-eds rehashing the same debates, long comment threads that always seemed to spiral into noise. I scrolled quickly, half engaged, until one post stopped me cold.

"Stand With the Jewish People. Harvard University. December 10, 2023."

That was all it said. Just a simple flyer—black text, plain background, time and place. No glossy graphics, no bold colors, no hashtags. But for me, it might as well have been a bugle call. A summons.

Harvard. That wasn't just any campus. By then it had become ground zero for the antisemitism epidemic in Massachusetts. The stories coming out of Cambridge were sickening: Jewish students harassed and spat on, excluded from study groups, shouted down in classrooms. Flyers and graffiti telling them to "go back to Poland." Professors twisting lectures into political theater that painted Jews as oppressors. And through it all, administrators looked the other way, hiding behind cowardly statements about "complex issues" and "free expression."

These weren't distant headlines. They were happening a few miles from where I grew up, on the same streets I had walked as a young man. Kids—because that's what they still were, kids in hoodies and backpacks—couldn't walk to class without being told they were complicit in crimes thousands of miles away. They weren't asked their views. Their very existence as Jews was treated as an indictment.

I could feel my chest tighten as I read. Rage mixed with something deeper—disbelief, betrayal. This was Harvard. The self-proclaimed crown jewel of higher education, a place that never missed an opportunity to lecture the world about tolerance, diversity, and inclusion. They draped rainbow flags across their gates. They organized vigils for every cause under the sun. But when it came to Jews? Silence. Worse than silence—excuses. Hypocrisy so naked it made my stomach turn.

I stared at the flyer on my screen for a long time. The simplicity of it struck me. No polished slogans, no PR spin. Just a call: *Stand With the Jewish People.*

I closed my laptop and sat back on my couch. My coffee had gone cold, but I didn't notice. The decision was already made. I was going to Cambridge.

It wasn't even a choice, really. It was instinct. The same instinct that had carried me through Bosnia, Kosovo, Iraq. The same fire that had burned in me on October 7 when I had wanted nothing more than to put a uniform back on and fight shoulder to shoulder with the IDF. If I couldn't be there,

I would be here. If I couldn't stand on the frontlines in Israel, then I would stand on the frontlines in Massachusetts.

December 10 wasn't just a date on a flyer. It was a line in the sand.

Harvard, December 10

The morning of December 10 was gray and wet, the kind of New England day that seeps into your bones even if the thermometer insists it isn't freezing. A fine, relentless rain drifted down in sheets—not a storm, not a downpour, just that stubborn drizzle that soaks you through all the same. The streets of Cambridge glistened, slick with puddles and streaked with the red and yellow blur of brake lights.

I parked a few blocks away, zipped my jacket to the top, and started walking. The flyer I had seen online was folded in my pocket, though I no longer needed it. Its words were etched into me now: *Stand With the Jewish People. Harvard University. December 10, 2023.*

As I approached Harvard, my stomach tightened. I didn't know what I was walking into. Maybe there would be a crowd of students chanting in counter-protest, their faces twisted with rage. Maybe there would be only a handful of people, swallowed by the silence of a campus that didn't care. Maybe—my worst fear—there would be no one at all. Just me, standing awkwardly in the rain, a soldier without a unit.

But when I turned the corner into the square, there was someone.

One man. Alone.

He stood tall, holding two flags—one American, one Israeli. Their colors snapped in the damp wind, bright against the washed-out gray sky. In front of him, propped on the monument, was an oil menorah. The rain beaded and streaked its metal, but he stood to adjust it carefully, shielding the wicks with his hands. I knew who he was the instant I saw him.

The Flag Guy.

I had followed his presence online without realizing it. Photos of him had circulated for months: one man with two flags, standing silently at rallies and vigils, sometimes with hundreds of angry faces shouting around him. He didn't hide. He didn't cower. He just showed up. A single figure of defiance and resilience.

And now here he was, in Cambridge, lighting a menorah in the rain.

I walked up, introduced myself. He nodded, smiled faintly, then turned back to the task at hand. The menorah leaned slightly, imperfect on the monument, but it stood. When he lit the first candle, the flame sputtered and wavered in the drizzle, but it held.

Hanukkah. The festival of lights. Jews around the world were kindling menorahs that week, remembering the Maccabees, remembering survival against impossible odds. And here, in the heart of one of the most prestigious universities in the world, two men stood in the rain with a menorah—on a campus where Jewish students were harassed, spat on, shouted down, told that being Jewish was itself a crime.

Something about it felt holy. The contrast was sharp as glass: light against darkness, defiance against fear, presence against erasure.

We stood there for hours as the rain fell. He told me stories—not to brag, but because they poured out of him the way conviction does when it's lived, not theorized. Stories of rallies where he had been completely alone, holding those same two flags while crowds chanted "From the river to the sea." Stories of students passing by who whispered *thank you* so softly he barely heard them, afraid to be seen even speaking to him. Stories of mobs that jeered, of voices that called for his death, of nights when he went home soaked, exhausted, but certain that showing up had mattered.

What struck me most wasn't bitterness. He wasn't angry, at least not in the way I expected. His words carried something else—clarity. He knew why he was there. He knew that silence was complicity. And he believed, with a kind of quiet stubbornness, that standing in the open mattered more than shouting slogans.

At one point he paused, glanced at me, and said something that lodged deep inside me:

"Sometimes the most powerful thing you can do is just stand. Don't hide. Don't apologize. Just be visible."

Those words hit harder than any speech, harder than any rallying cry. They were simple, almost understated, but they cut straight to the core. For me, as a soldier, standing had always been tactical—take your post, hold the line, man the wire. But this was different. This was moral standing. Human standing. Standing not just as a presence, but as a refusal to disappear.

I left Harvard Yard soaked to the skin, but something inside me burned steady and warm. I had come looking for a rally. What I found was a menorah sputtering in the rain, a man with two flags, and a lesson that would shape everything I did from that day forward.

I walked back to my car with my hood pulled tight, rain dripping from the brim, the December cold settling into my bones. But inside I wasn't cold at all. Something had lit up in me, something steady and undeniable. The image of that menorah, flickering stubbornly against the drizzle, wouldn't leave my mind. Neither would his words: *"Sometimes the most powerful thing you can do is just stand."*

That night, when I got home, I didn't just scroll. I didn't just shake my head at the headlines or curse under my breath at the cowardice of politicians. I pulled out my phone and started looking for the next rally. The next vigil. The next time Jews would gather to say they weren't going to be erased.

I thought of the survivor who had shown us his tattoo back in middle school. I thought of Bosnia, of mass graves uncovered in mud. I thought of Henry Risner's casket draped in a flag. I thought of October 7, of paragliders cutting across the sky, of children murdered in their beds while the world shrugged.

And I thought of that lone man in Harvard Yard, holding two flags in the rain.

It wasn't enough anymore to rage at home. It wasn't enough to post online or argue over coffee. I had spent a lifetime learning that silence is complicity, that absence is permission. If Jews in Massachusetts were going to stand, then so was I.

I wasn't a student. I wasn't a rabbi. I wasn't a politician. I was just one man. But I had been a soldier once, and I knew the power of showing up. I knew what it meant to take a post and hold it. To say with your body: *I am here. I won't move.*

That's when the decision crystallized. I wasn't going to sit on the sidelines anymore. The fight had come to my backyard, and I would answer it the way I always had—by standing. By being visible. By refusing to let the flicker of light be snuffed out.

From that rainy night in Cambridge forward, everything shifted. I wasn't just a supporter of Israel in principle. I was a man in the square, on the street, in the yard, shoulder to shoulder with those who refused to hide.

And I knew, in the marrow of my bones, that this was only the beginning.

Reflection:

Looking back now, I can trace the line as if it were carved in stone. October 7 lit the fire. December 10 gave it form.

That morning in my living room, coffee in hand, scrolling through footage of Jews being butchered in their homes, I felt rage like I hadn't felt since Iraq. It was the same heat that had surged in me when I saw villages razed in Bosnia, when I carried my best friend's body home from war. But rage, by itself, is directionless. It burns, it sears, it consumes—but it doesn't lead.

December 10 changed that. Standing at Harvard, soaked by rain, watching a menorah flicker stubbornly against the storm, I realized that fire could be turned into light. The anger didn't have to just eat me alive—it could be channeled into action. Into showing up. Into refusing silence.

That day was a line in the sand for me. Before, I had spoken about Israel in conversations with friends, on social media, in quiet circles. Afterwards, I spoke with my feet, my presence, my voice in the open air. Loudly. Proudly. Visibly.

Because the world had gone mad. I saw student groups in the most prestigious universities of this country excuse rape and murder as "resistance." I saw protesters paint murals of paragliders as if the slaughter of kids at a music festival was some kind of heroic act. I saw politicians hide behind cowardly half-truths, too afraid to say the obvious: this was evil. And when the world starts excusing evil, silence isn't neutrality—it's betrayal.

But I wasn't confused. I knew exactly where I stood. I stood with Israel. I stood with the Jewish people. I stood with the kids in Cambridge who were spat on while walking to class, with the parents in Tel Aviv who tucked their children into bomb shelters, with every person who carried the torch of survival in the face of hatred.

And I understood something else that day: it doesn't take thousands to begin a stand. It takes one. One man holding two flags in the rain. One menorah burning in the dark. One choice is to stop scrolling and start showing up.

For me, it began in Cambridge, beside a stranger who had already been carrying the flame long before I arrived. The fire that October 7 ignited was no longer just rage. It had become resolve.

Chapter 10:

Stars and Stripes — Star of David

Maynard, Massachusetts. A quiet mill town tucked away in Middlesex County, better known for its painted murals and small-town charm than for conflict. But for me, it became something else entirely—a personal Lexington and Concord. Not because muskets fired or redcoats marched, but because the square itself became a battleground for truth. Just a short drive from the soil where the American Revolution began, I found myself fighting my own revolution—this time against lies, hatred, and intimidation.

I never planned for Maynard to be the place. But by early 2024, I had reached my breaking point. Every Saturday, a pro-terrorist group claimed the town square. They waved Palestinian flags, chanted slogans, and filled the air with rhetoric that boiled down to one message: Jews should not exist. Week after week, they occupied public space unchallenged. Their voices grew bolder, not because they were right, but because no one stood against them. To me, it was no different than Nazis gathering in a square eighty years ago. The language had changed, the branding updated with hashtags and slogans, but the ideology was the same. Erasure disguised as activism. Hatred dressed up as "resistance."

So one night, I typed a message into one of the antisemitism-fighting groups I had joined after October 7. Just one line, nothing fancy, but charged with intent: *"I'm going to counter protest in Maynard. Who's coming with me?"* I hit send, not knowing if anyone would answer. Maybe I'd be alone again, like I had been at Harvard with The Flag Guy. But even if it came down to that, I knew I had to go.

That first Saturday the skies opened up. Of course they did. Just like at Harvard, the weather seemed determined to test me. Cold rain fell in thin sheets, soaking everything, seeping into my jacket, running down the poles of the flags I carried. When I pulled up, I spotted them instantly—about ten protesters clustered together under umbrellas and ponchos. Palestinian flags draped across shoulders, fists pumping the air, signs lifted high: *"End the Occupation!" "From the River to the Sea!" "Intifada Now!"* Their chants carried across the slick pavement, sharp and practiced.

I parked, stepped out, and grabbed my two flags—American and Israeli. Planting my boots firmly in front of them in the square, I raised them high and let the fabric snap in the wind. The effect was immediate. Their rhythm broke. Chants faltered. Heads turned. They hadn't expected resistance—certainly not someone bold enough to stand directly in front of them with the very symbols they despised waving defiantly in the rain. I didn't shout back. I didn't argue. I simply stood. Presence itself was my weapon.

Cars rolled past—some honked in support, a few drivers glared. My hands were frozen around the poles, my jacket plastered to my skin, but I didn't move. For an hour, I held those flags steady. The square that had been theirs alone was no longer uncontested. It was shared ground now.

Forty minutes in, I heard footsteps approaching. A woman, local, middle-aged, determined expression. She looked from me to them and back again. "You here for them?" she asked, nodding toward the protesters. I shook my head. "No. I'm here for Israel." "Good," she said simply. Then she pulled an umbrella from her bag, popped it open, and stood right beside me. Her presence was a spark. I hadn't realized the weight of solitude until someone else chose to shoulder it with me. We didn't exchange names, not yet. It didn't matter. She saw what was happening in her own town, felt the same sickness, and decided to act. There were two of us now. Two flags. Two voices of defiance in the rain.

The next Saturday, I came back. So did she. This time, a man from a neighboring town joined us—he had seen my post online. The week after that, another came. Then another. It wasn't a flood, but it was a steady trickle. Sometimes we were just three or four, standing against their ten. Other times, we matched them. And on our best days, we outnumbered them outright.

The atmosphere shifted. What had been a stage for their unchallenged slogans became a square contested by two narratives—one of hate, one of resilience. You could see the irritation in their faces. Their chants grew louder, their signs bigger, their cameras trained on us as if hoping to catch us slipping. But no matter what they threw, we didn't flinch. Flags high. Feet steady. Rain, snow, or sun—we showed up. Week by week, Maynard was no longer just theirs. It was ours too. And with every Saturday that passed, the message grew stronger: Jews would not stand alone.

One weekday evening, my phone rang. It was the Maynard police. The officer's voice was cautious, rehearsed almost, the way someone speaks when they're trying not to ignite a spark. "Mr. Hayes," he began, "we've received some complaints. Apparently, you've made a number of people uncomfortable by taking their photos during the demonstrations."

For a moment I thought I had misheard. Uncomfortable? After weeks of standing across from people chanting "Intifada now," waving flags that celebrated terror, after listening to slogans that denied Israel's right to exist, *was my camera* the problem? I almost laughed.

"Good," I said flatly, the word coming out harder than I intended. "It's not my job to make them comfortable. It's my right to document public demonstrations in a public square. If they want to feel safe, they can stay home."

There was silence on the other end, the officer weighing his words. "Well, technically, you're not breaking any laws…"

"Exactly," I cut in. "And I'll continue to stand proudly with Israel and the Jewish people in Maynard. Every Saturday. Rain or shine."

That was the end of it. They knew, and I knew, that I wasn't out there to provoke violence or cross any legal line. I was there to shine a light on the truth, to make sure hate didn't go unchallenged in the heart of a small New England town.

And the truth is, the endurance worked. At first, their group was consistent—ten, sometimes fifteen people, chanting for an hour as if repetition could make their slogans true. But after weeks of us showing up opposite them, something shifted. Their energy began to sag. Their numbers shrank. Weekly protests turned to every other week. Then monthly. And then—silence.

We hadn't shouted them down. We hadn't tried to intimidate them. We had simply outlasted them. By showing up, by planting flags in the rain and heat, by refusing to cede the square, we won. What had begun as one man standing alone with soaked flags became something else entirely: a small kibbutz of resistance, right in the heart of Massachusetts.

The lesson was seared into me. Presence works. You don't need a crowd of thousands. You don't need a bullhorn. You need courage, consistency, and the willingness to be visible. That's enough to tilt the ground beneath the feet of those who thrive on intimidation.

Maynard taught me something else, too—that I wasn't alone. There were others out there, just like me. People who felt the fire inside but hadn't yet found a way to channel it. People are tired of scrolling past antisemitism on social media. People are tired of whispering their support for Israel in private. People are tired of being silenced by fear. All it took was one flag, one person refusing to bow, to give them permission to step forward.

That was the blueprint. If it could happen in Maynard, it could happen anywhere. One town at a time, one flag at a time, public space could be reclaimed. Hate could be contested. The silence could be broken.

And from that point on, I knew exactly what I was meant to do.

In April 2024, I took a short break from activism to fly down to Florida. It wasn't for politics, it wasn't for protests. It was for something simpler—something I'd always wanted to do: the Star Wars experience at Hollywood Studios.

I've been a Star Wars nerd for as long as I can remember. The saga was more than movies; it was mythology. The clash of good and evil, rebellion against empire, hope surviving against impossible odds—it all carried meaning that stuck with me long after the credits rolled. And by then, after months of standing with flags in the rain and confronting lies head-on, Star Wars felt even more personal. The Rebellion wasn't just fiction. It was a mirror.

When I packed for the trip, I pulled a shirt from my drawer: black cotton, bold blue Star of David across the chest. No ambiguity, no subtlety—just a declaration. I knew it would draw looks, and that was the point.

From the moment I stepped into TF Green Airport in Providence, the stares began. Side glances from fellow passengers. A scowl from a man at the coffee counter. Another man muttered something under his breath, then flipped me off as I walked past. My response was always the same: a smile and a "Thank you—have a great day." If a piece of fabric could rattle them, it said more about their hate than about my courage.

By the time I landed in Orlando and made my way to Disney's Hollywood Studios, the shirt had already become a conversation starter. A couple of strangers gave me quiet nods. One guy in line for security broke into a grin and slapped me on the shoulder, saying, "Respect, brother." Another high-fived me as we both shuffled toward the tram. It wasn't much, but in that sea of tourists, those gestures mattered.

Inside the park, surrounded by Jedi robes, stormtroopers, and kids wielding plastic lightsabers, I felt oddly at peace. The story of resistance was everywhere—Luke facing Vader, Leia refusing to bow, Han risking everything for his friends. Fiction, yes, but it carried truth. Good and evil are always in tension, and survival always depends on those willing to stand.

That evening, I wandered through Disney Springs, the shopping and dining hub filled with neon and music. It should have been carefree, but it wasn't. The place was packed with tourists from around the world, and I noticed more than a few Muslims eyeing me, their stares lingering on the Star of David across my chest. Some shook their heads. Others just looked in disbelief that I would wear something so brazen, so unapologetic, in public. A few even muttered as I walked past. But I didn't flinch. If anything, their stares only hardened my resolve. I wasn't going to shrink to make them comfortable.

Before flying home, I ordered a second shirt online—white, with the Israeli flag front and center, beneath it the words in bold Hebrew: *Am Yisrael Chai*. That phrase wasn't just a slogan. It was a declaration that after every exile, every pogrom, every genocide, the Jewish people still endure. And by wearing it, I was adding my voice to that chorus.

At the Orlando airport check-in counter, I stood behind a woman traveling with her two daughters. She glanced at my shirt, then looked me in the eye. "Thank you," she said softly.

We started to talk. She told me her older daughter—maybe eleven or twelve—had been having a terrible year in school back in New Jersey. Bullied almost daily for being Jewish. Teased, isolated, made to feel like an outsider in her own country.

When the girls came back from the restroom, I reached into my backpack and pulled out a bracelet. Handmade by a friend in New York, strung with blue and white beads, stamped with words I believed in: *I Stand With the IDF*. I handed it to the girl. She looked down at it, then up at me, her eyes wet with gratitude. Her mother hugged me like we'd known each other for years.

That was the power of visibility. Not just confronting haters, but reminding those who feel alone that they are not. A t-shirt. A bracelet. A moment of solidarity in an airport terminal. Small things, maybe—but for that family, it meant the world. And for me, it reinforced a truth I'd already learned in Maynard and Harvard: silence helps no one. Presence changes everything.

When I returned to Massachusetts, the fight picked up again.

Every Thursday, protesters gathered outside Congressman Jake Auchincloss's office in Newton, a heavily Jewish suburb. Their numbers were usually twenty or more, waving Palestinian flags, shouting slogans, and staging the same tired theater I had already seen in Maynard and on campuses across the state. They wanted visibility, legitimacy, and control of the narrative.

I decided to join—not to argue, not to fight, but to stand. To be present. To make sure that anyone passing by saw at least one person holding the

Stars and Stripes and the Star of David, not just the green, red, and black of people celebrating Hamas's cause.

The first time I showed up, I noticed something new: the so-called Jewish Voice for Peace marshals. They wore reflective vests, their faces half-hidden by masks and sunglasses. They didn't hold signs or lead chants. Their jobs were different. They formed human walls along the sidewalk, using silence and posture as weapons. Their purpose was clear: block dissent, silence opposition, and intimidate anyone who dared stand against them.

I walked slowly with my two flags, back and forth across the sidewalk, the fabric snapping in the wind. Most of the crowd shouted their usual slogans, but one person stepped out of formation, shoving a Palestinian flag in my face. He waved it inches from my nose, taunting, trying to break my calm.

Without raising my voice, I snatched the flag, yanked it off the pole, tossed it to the ground, and planted my boot squarely on it.

"You're not going to do that to me," I said evenly.

The air shifted. The chants faltered. For a second, you could feel the uncertainty ripple through them. Another marshal stepped closer, close enough to breathe on me, his eyes glaring above the mask. I laughed in his face.

"You don't scare me," I told him. "You never will."

Their response was predictable: they called the police. That was their playbook—provoke, record, cry foul, and hope to flip the narrative.

When the officer arrived, he asked for everyone's version of events, then watched the footage. After a pause, he looked at them, then at me. "No laws were broken," he said simply. He asked me to give them a few feet of space, and I agreed. I've always respected law enforcement. But the message was clear: I wasn't going anywhere.

From that day forward, the dynamic shifted. They knew me now. They recognized me. They even gave me a nickname, plastered on the internet and repeated with a sneer: *The Lone Zionist Aggressor.*

I wore it like a badge of honor.

Over the weeks, something else began to happen. My presence became familiar—not just to the pro-Israel supporters who occasionally joined me, but to the anti-Israel crowd as well. They would spot me across town squares or at other protests, their voices tightening, their body language shifting. They knew I would show up, rain or shine, and that unnerved them.

Slowly, they began hiding their own faces more and more. Keffiyehs pulled higher, masks cinched tighter, sunglasses covering their eyes. It struck me as pathetic. If you believe in what you're shouting—"Intifada now," "From the river to the sea"—why hide? Why cower behind fabric?

The truth is, deep down, they knew. They weren't fighting for liberation or justice. They were fighting for hate. And hate rarely wants to show its face in the light.

Reflection:

This chapter of my life wasn't something I had planned. I never set out to be an activist. I didn't dream of becoming a public figure. But sometimes, times choose you.

I had stood in Maynard's rain, refusing to give ground. I had handed a bracelet to a bullied Jewish girl in an airport. I had stared down masked marshals in Newton who thought intimidation would silence me. And through it all, I discovered the same truth over and over again: presence matters.

It isn't just about Israel. It's about the truth. About standing when it would be easier to sit. About making sure that hate doesn't get the last word.

One flag at a time, one town at a time, we were reclaiming public ground. And I had no plans to stop.

Chapter 11:

Brotherhood in Black Hats — Embraced in Faith

When I look back over the last few years, I can pinpoint certain moments that changed everything—turning points that shifted not just what I was doing, but who I was becoming. One of those moments came in the form of a simple phone call.

It was shortly after I had begun stepping into the public square, raising flags, confronting antisemitism, and lending my voice wherever I could. I was still raw then—raw with anger, raw with conviction, raw with the sense that silence was no longer acceptable. I hadn't yet thought of myself as anything other than an ally. Just a man trying to do his part.

And then my phone rang.

On the other end was a voice I didn't recognize: warm, confident, steady, with a hint of curiosity. "This is Rabbi Moshe Bleich," he said, "from Wellesley-Weston Chabad. I've been hearing about you."

I froze for a moment. A rabbi? Calling me? I wasn't Jewish. I had never set foot in a synagogue in my life, except maybe once as a guest. I braced myself for skepticism, maybe even suspicion. Surely this was going to be a polite but firm inquiry into who exactly I thought I was, parading around with Israeli flags and speaking out as if I had some right to.

But that wasn't what I heard.

Instead, he said: "I want to meet you. I want to understand what's driving you. And I think you should come by."

That invitation—simple, direct, and genuine—became the spark for a journey I never expected.

When I arrived at Chabad of Wellesley-Weston, I wasn't sure what to expect. A synagogue? A lecture hall? Some kind of office space? What I found was a warm, unpretentious building that felt more like a home than an institution. The smell of books, the faint aroma of food from a recent meal, the quiet hum of life—it was different from any religious space I had known before.

Rabbi Bleich greeted me at the door with a big smile and a handshake that was both firm and welcoming. His energy hit me immediately—dynamic, almost electric, but grounded by an authenticity you couldn't fake. He radiated the sense that he had been waiting for me, not out of obligation, but because he genuinely wanted to know my story.

We sat down together, just the two of us, and he wasted no time cutting to the heart of things. "So," he said, leaning forward slightly, "who are you? Why do you do what you do?"

The question caught me off guard. Not because I hadn't asked it of myself before, but because no one had ever asked me so plainly, without judgment or pretense.

So I told him. I told him my story. About my upbringing in Brookline, my military service in Bosnia, Kosovo, and Iraq. About the funerals I had attended, the graves I had seen, the hatred I had witnessed firsthand. About October 7, about standing with flags in the rain, about deciding that silence was no longer an option. I told him I wasn't Jewish, that I had no plans to convert, but that I felt something in my soul pulling me toward this fight—a conviction that defending Israel and the Jewish people wasn't just "their" issue. It was a human issue. A moral one.

He listened. Really listened. Not with the polite nods of someone waiting to speak, but with the intensity of someone who wanted to understand every word. His eyes didn't wander. He didn't check his phone or glance at a clock. He gave me the rare gift of full attention, the kind that makes you hear yourself more clearly as you speak.

When I finished, he smiled again. "You know," he said, "you may not be Jewish, but you're carrying something very Jewish in your heart."

That line stuck with me. Because it didn't feel like flattery. It felt like recognition. Like he had named something in me I had never dared to name myself.

Over the course of that first conversation, and in the many that followed, I began to realize that Rabbi Bleich was unlike anyone I had ever known. A dynamo of Judaism, yes, but more than that—a man who embodied his faith with joy, conviction, and warmth. He didn't preach to me. He didn't hand me a list of commandments or insist I change my life. Instead, he opened a door. "Come in," he seemed to say, "ask your questions, share your story, and let's walk together."

I had grown used to religion being about judgment, about who measured up and who didn't. But with him, it was the opposite. He wasn't interested in excluding anyone. He was interested in lifting everyone.

And that, I would come to learn, is the essence of Chabad.

From that first meeting, the doors kept opening. What began as a handshake and a conversation in Wellesley quickly became an invitation into something much larger than I had imagined. I was invited to gatherings—not just formal lectures, but casual conversations, holiday events, and community meals that seemed to unfold as naturally as breathing.

Walking into those spaces for the first time, I half-expected to feel like an outsider, the lone non-Jew in a sea of shared history and ritual. But the opposite happened. I wasn't asked to explain myself. I wasn't asked to prove anything. Nobody quizzed me about my motives or measured me against a checklist of beliefs. Instead, people shook my hand, passed me plates of kugel and challah, laughed with me around the table, and even asked me to share about my activism.

The first time I stood before a room full of men and women who lived the reality of antisemitism every day, I felt my throat tighten. These weren't abstract "communities" I had been defending in public squares; they were flesh and blood, parents and students and grandparents, people who had felt the sting of hatred in grocery stores, classrooms, and workplaces. And yet they wanted to hear from me—a non-Jew, a veteran, someone whose conviction came not from ancestry but from moral clarity. Standing there, telling them about the rallies I'd attended, the hate I'd witnessed, the flags I had carried, I realized I wasn't speaking to strangers. I was speaking to my family, even if we had only just met. And the way they welcomed me—as an ally, sometimes even as a brother—humbled me in ways I can't fully describe.

Through Chabad, the introductions multiplied. I met IDF soldiers visiting Massachusetts who spoke not in abstract slogans but in raw, human terms: about the friends they had lost, the nights they hadn't slept, the strength they still found to lace their boots and report for duty the next day. I met survivors of October 7th who carried trauma in their eyes but steel in their voices—ordinary people who had lived through unspeakable horror and still insisted on living with dignity and faith. I met students navigating the hostility of campuses that should have nurtured them, but instead treated them like pariahs. They told me about classrooms where professors excused terror, about dormitories where mezuzot were ripped from doorframes, about social circles that evaporated overnight because they refused to disavow Israel.

Each encounter reshaped my understanding of Jewish endurance. These weren't abstract stories of resilience; they were living testimonies. And with each person I met, my own conviction deepened. I realized that my fight wasn't just symbolic. It mattered. It gave breath and visibility to people who often felt unseen, unheard, and alone.

What struck me most was the paradox: there were people who had every reason to retreat inward, to harden their hearts against a hostile world, and yet they chose the opposite. They chose to welcome me. To invite. To trust. And in doing so, they didn't just pull me deeper into their community—they gave me a model of courage that was as defiant as it was generous.

What began with Rabbi Bleich in Wellesley soon expanded far beyond one shul or one conversation. Massachusetts, I discovered, was dotted with Chabad emissaries—each with his own style, his own rhythm, but all of them carrying the same unmistakable fire in their hearts.

There was Rabbi Yisroel Freeman of Chabad of Sudbury Massachusetts, joyous, a leader whose words carried weight precisely because he never wasted them. When he spoke, you leaned in, because you knew every sentence had intention.

Then there was Rabbi Yossi Lipsker of Chabad of the North Shore, steady and grounded, with a wild side, playing guitar or dancing away.

In Chabad of Chestnut Hill, Rabbi Uminer greeted me with kindness that disarmed everyone who crossed his path. He was, in the truest sense, a mensch—someone whose warmth reminded you that goodness itself could be a kind of power.

From Newton, Rabbi Prus brought sharp insight and approachable warmth, weaving tradition and modern sensibility with a kind of quiet brilliance. He had the gift of making even the most complex ideas feel accessible.

Rabbi Dan Rodkin at Shaloh House in Brighton embodied another side of the mission—somehow blending tradition with modern outreach in a way that felt seamless. He could hold a Torah scroll in one hand and a smartphone in the other without contradiction, showing that Judaism had a place in every generation.

And then there was Rabbi Barber, Chabad of Beverly-Salem newer to the Massachusetts community, bringing with him an energy that was almost contagious. He radiated positivity in a way that made people smile before he even opened his mouth.

What struck me was that none of them treated me as an outsider. None of them asked what a non-Jew was doing in their orbit, or measured me against some litmus test of belonging. Instead, they welcomed me as someone searching, someone trying, someone reaching for something higher.

As I moved from Wellesley to Sudbury, from Brighton to the North Shore, I began to see the bigger picture. Chabad wasn't just a collection of rabbis or a network of synagogues. It was a movement—one that stretched across Massachusetts, across the United States, across the globe. And somehow, without planning it, I was being pulled into its orbit.

There's a saying in the Jewish world: the Chabad door is always open.

At first, I thought it was just a metaphor—something nice people said to capture a spirit of hospitality. But then I walked through those doors myself and realized it wasn't a slogan. It was literal. Any Chabad house, anywhere in the world, would welcome you. It didn't matter if you were Orthodox or secular, deeply observant or barely questioning, Jew or gentile. If you walked in, you belonged.

That was my experience from the very first day. I hadn't converted. I hadn't adopted rituals I didn't fully understand. I was still the same man who had grown up in Brookline, who had walked past that Lubavitch sign for years without knowing what it meant. To me back then, it was just another piece of neighborhood scenery—like the corner store or the old brick schoolhouse. Now I know better. That sign meant home. Not home in the sense of heritage or bloodline, but home in the sense of light—a light that didn't ask for credentials before it warmed you.

And that's the thing about light: once it's shared, it belongs to everyone it touches.

As my connection with local rabbis deepened—first Rabbi Bleich in Wellesley, then Rabbi Lipsker in Swampscott, Rabbi Uminer in Chestnut Hill, and others—I began to notice a common thread weaving through all of them. Whether it was a line in conversation, a story told over a meal, or a quiet reference during prayer, the same name kept surfacing: the Rebbe.

At first, it was subtle. A quote dropped into a teaching. An anecdote recalled with a smile. But the way they spoke of him caught my attention. To them, Rabbi Menachem Mendel Schneerson wasn't just a historical figure from the past. He wasn't a photograph on a wall or a leader confined to memory. He was alive in their work, in their mission, in their words. The Rebbe was present in the way they lived.

Curiosity got the better of me. I began searching for him on my own. I found grainy videos online of his farbrengens—those legendary gatherings where he would teach, bless, sing, and inspire. The footage might have been decades old, but his presence cut through the blur of VHS and static. There he was: a bearded man in a black fedora, speaking with fire, with compassion, with a calm authority that seemed to reach past the camera and into the heart of anyone listening.

I read his letters, each one brimming with precision and care. I bought books that collected his talks, his philosophy, his vision. I listened to lectures about him, trying to piece together why this man, above all others, had become the anchor for Chabad's global movement. And slowly, the picture became clear.

The Rebbe wasn't just a rabbi. He was a visionary who had taken a relatively small Hasidic group in Brooklyn and transformed it into one of the most far-reaching Jewish networks in the world. But more than the scale of his success, it was the substance of his message that struck me. He didn't build walls; he built bridges. He didn't demand perfection; he demanded effort. His philosophy was radical in its simplicity: every Jew mattered, and every action mattered, no matter how small.

One line of his hit me like a lightning bolt: *"In a hall of perfect darkness, if you light one small candle, its light will be seen from afar. Its precious light will be seen by everyone."*

That sentence could have been written for me. It was exactly what I felt I had been doing—standing in places where darkness reigned, raising a flag, showing up when it was easier to stay home, trying to light even a single candle against the storm.

The Rebbe's words gave shape to what I had been groping toward without knowing it. They told me it wasn't about grand gestures or sweeping victories. It was about presence. About faithfulness. About one small act of courage that, in the right moment, could cut through a sea of shadows.

Through Chabad, and through the Rebbe, I began to realize that the path I was walking wasn't just about activism. It was about something deeper: light, dignity, endurance. And even though I wasn't Jewish, those teachings didn't shut me out—they invited me in.

As I studied more, I found elements of Chabad philosophy that spoke directly to me as a non-Jew, ideas that didn't just sit on a page but connected to scars and memories I carried from war zones, funerals, and activism.

Ahavat Yisrael — Love for Every Jew. This principle of unconditional love hit me with force because I had seen the opposite too many times. In Bosnia, Kosovo, and Iraq, I had watched people slaughter each other over differences—neighbors turned against neighbors because of ethnicity, tribe, or religion. Hatred thrived on division. Chabad's insistence on embracing every Jew, regardless of observance or background, was revolutionary in its simplicity. It wasn't about purity tests, it wasn't about who was "religious enough." It was love without conditions. And to me, having seen the cost of division, that kind of radical unity felt like the antidote to the world's sickness.

Joy in Worship. I had grown up with religion framed as obligation, duty, even guilt. Faith was often presented like a ledger—sins against virtues, commandments kept against those broken. With Chabad, I saw something altogether different. Worship wasn't heavy; it was alive. Singing, dancing, clapping hands at a Shabbat table—it wasn't performance, it was joy spilling over. This wasn't religion as a burden. This was faith as life, faith as music, faith as light. For someone who had carried so much weight—of war, of trauma, of grief—the idea that joy itself could be holy was transformative.

Action Matters. The Rebbe taught that even the smallest mitzvah, the smallest good deed, carried cosmic weight. That teaching landed hard for me because I had lived both sides of it. In combat, I had seen how the smallest actions—checking a corner, adjusting formation, offering a sip of water to a child—could ripple into life or death. And later, in activism, I thought of the bracelet I had given to that young girl at the airport. Five dollars' worth of beads, but it gave her armor to face a hostile world. Chabad validated that instinct in me: that small acts matter. They are not insignificant. They are world-changing in ways we may never see.

Purpose. Perhaps the most powerful idea I found in Chabad was its insistence that every soul has a mission in this world. That struck me like a personal revelation. I had wandered through so many landscapes—Bosnia's ruins, Kosovo's graves, Iraq's chaos, and later, the protests and town squares of Massachusetts. At times I had wondered if it all added up to anything, or if my life was just a collection of scars. But Chabad told me otherwise. It told me that none of it was random. That my experiences, my choices, even my pain were threads in a larger tapestry. That my mission wasn't an accident—I had been placed here, at this moment in history, for a reason.

The more I immersed myself in Chabad, the more I began to feel it wasn't just supplementing my activism—it was grounding it. Advocacy had given me a mission, but Chabad gave me a compass. It reminded me that the fight against antisemitism wasn't only about politics or rallies. It was about dignity, truth, and light. It was about ensuring that every Jew could live openly, proudly, without fear, in their own homeland and in their own neighborhoods.

And through it all, even though I wasn't Jewish, Chabad never made me feel like an outsider. They didn't push conversion. They didn't test my motives. They simply welcomed me as a fellow traveler on the road of purpose. That kind of inclusivity is rare in religious spaces, and it left a mark on me. For someone who had felt like an outsider in so many places—from battlefields to small-town squares—Chabad's open door was more than hospitality. It was healing.

At first, I used the word "Chabadnik" as a joke. It was a shorthand, a way of telling people, "Yeah, I spend a lot of time with Chabad now," without having to unpack the whole story. But the more I said it, the less it felt like a joke and the more it felt like the truth. I wasn't Jewish. I hadn't gone through a conversion. I hadn't suddenly rewritten my identity. But something deeper was happening. Spiritually, philosophically, emotionally—I was orbiting Chabad. Their values were becoming my values. Their teachings were becoming my compass.

It wasn't about wearing a label. It was about recognizing what was already happening inside me. Over time, I realized I wasn't borrowing their light for a momentary cause; I was carrying it forward in my own life. Calling myself a Chabadnik wasn't roleplay or flattery. It was acknowledgment: this movement had changed me, and its imprint was etched into how I stood, spoke, and lived.

The transformation didn't happen in a vacuum. It happened in living rooms filled with the smell of fresh-baked challah and chicken soup. It happened around long Shabbat tables where voices rose in song, where laughter competed with clinking glasses, where joy wasn't an accessory but the foundation of faith itself. It happened in quiet conversations with rabbis who answered my hardest questions without judgment, and in louder ones where kids ran around, singing snatches of Hebrew songs they barely understood but knew by heart.

What struck me most wasn't just theology—it was the way they lived. In a world obsessed with division, Chabad insisted on unity. In a culture drowning in cynicism, Chabad insisted on joy. In an age of apathy, Chabad insisted on action. And in a time when so many treat people as disposable, Chabad insisted on dignity. These weren't abstract ideals. They were woven into the way candles were lit on Friday nights, the way blessings were said over wine, the way people were greeted at the door no matter what they looked like or where they came from.

Those values resonated because I had seen their opposites. I had seen division rip Bosnia apart, cynicism poison Iraq, apathy let genocide unfold in Kosovo. I have seen what happens when human dignity is erased, when people are reduced to labels and enemies. And here, in Chabad houses across Massachusetts, I found the antidote. Not policy. Not politics. But people who insisted that every act of kindness mattered, every soul mattered, every bit of light mattered.

That's why I began to feel at home among Chabadniks. Not because I was born into it, but because it reflected the kind of human being I wanted to be. Their joy gave me strength. Their discipline gave me direction. Their love for every Jew widened my sense of humanity. Their philosophy gave me something I had long been missing: peace with purpose.

So yes, I call myself a Chabadnik now. Not out of performance, not as a gimmick, and certainly not to curry favor. I use that word because it captures something essential about my evolution. Chabad found me when I wasn't looking. It welcomed me when I could have been dismissed. It gave me wisdom when I was burning with rage. It gave me joy when I was weary. It gave me purpose when I needed it most.

I didn't set out to find Chabad. But Chabad, somehow, found me—in the songs, in the teachings, in the smiles of children, in the quiet conviction of rabbis, in the light of Shabbat candles that somehow seemed to burn against every storm. And for that, I'll be forever grateful.

Chapter 12:

The Gathering Storm — Darkness Approaches

The summer of 2024 was unlike anything I had experienced before. While most people were soaking in the New England sun, planning beach trips or backyard cookouts, I spent nearly every weekend confronting a wave of antisemitic activism cloaked in anti-war slogans. For most, summer meant ice cream trucks and ballgames; for me, it meant flags, protests, police tape, and a fight that felt like it would never end.

What started as anger over the war in Israel quickly metastasized into open hostility toward Jews in general. They weren't even trying to hide it anymore. Protest after protest proved that the hatred wasn't just about a conflict thousands of miles away—it was about us, our community, right here at home. It was in the chants, the signs, the sneers, and the threats hurled at anyone who dared to show up with an Israeli flag.

From Quincy to Lexington, Boston to Brookline, Newton to Plymouth, the streets of Massachusetts turned into battlegrounds of ideology. We weren't fighting over policy anymore—we were fighting for truth, for decency, for the right to exist without being demonized.

It was exhausting, relentless work. But silence was no longer an option.

Quincy quickly became one of the most volatile fronts. Their regulars showed up every week with the same slogans, the same keffiyehs, the same hatred. At first, it was shouting matches, chants versus chants. But then it escalated.

There was George, a familiar face—tall, broad-shouldered, with a permanent sneer. He wasn't content to just yell. He made threats, muttering things like, *"You won't be standing here long."* Once, he revved his engine and steered his car toward a group of my friends in a parking lot. The tires screeched, the smell of burning rubber filled the air, and for a split second, I thought we were about to witness a tragedy. He swerved at the last moment, laughing, as if it were a joke. But there was nothing funny about it.

And then there was Joe. Joe wasn't just another protester—he fancied himself a leader, a ringleader. He wore his socialist and communist credentials like a badge of honor, quoting Marx and Engels between rants about "colonizers" and "oppressors." His contempt for Jews and for Israel dripped from every word, barely concealed behind the veneer of "anti-war" rhetoric. What made it worse, almost grotesque, was his background. Joe wasn't some fringe character from the street. He had once been a public school teacher. He had sat on the retirement board of the Massachusetts Teachers Association.

That detail hit me like a brick. By then, the MTA had already revealed itself as one of the most antisemitic institutions in the state. They had issued statements condemning Israel while remaining silent about Hamas atrocities. They slipped anti-Israel talking points into professional development sessions. They supported resolutions dripping with bias, framing Jewish students as extensions of "colonial oppression." And here was Joe, a product of that very system, a man who had once been entrusted with teaching children, now spewing venom in the streets of Quincy.

It was all connected. The chants in Quincy, the resolutions passed by the MTA, the hostile campus climates—it was the same poison, just poured into different bottles. And Joe embodied it perfectly: a self-proclaimed intellectual who wielded ideology as a weapon, who cloaked old hatreds in new language, who turned his rage into a performance of "activism."

Quincy became my case study in how quickly words can curdle into threats, how quickly "anti-war" slogans can turn into open antisemitism. It wasn't just theory. It wasn't just politics. It was real. It was dangerous. And it was happening right in front of us.

The more time I spent in Quincy, the clearer it became that this wasn't just about one square in one town. It was about something bigger, something rotting from the inside of our institutions. Joe and his crew weren't inventing their rhetoric out of thin air. They were parroting it, amplifying it, regurgitating the same poisoned talking points being pushed by the Massachusetts Teachers Association and other so-called "progressive" groups that had long ago abandoned decency for ideology.

Every time I faced Joe in the square, I wasn't just confronting him. I was confronting the MTA, the professors on campuses who excused Hamas, the politicians who hedged instead of condemning murder. Joe was just their local representative—loud, smug, and unafraid to say the quiet part out loud.

That realization hardened my resolve. If I had once thought of my activism as showing up with flags to make sure Jews weren't standing alone, now I understood it as something broader: a fight against institutions that had normalized antisemitism under the cover of "social justice." The slogans I heard in Quincy were the same ones Jewish students were hearing on campuses across Massachusetts. The same ones Jewish teachers were whispering about in their staff rooms. The same ones Jewish parents feared their kids would be fed in classrooms.

I knew then that silence wasn't just dangerous—it was complicity. To stand down was to let Joe win, to let the MTA dictate the narrative, to let hatred masquerade as activism without challenge. So week after week, I showed up. Not just for the square, not just for the flags, but for the bigger fight. Because if Quincy taught me anything, it was that what starts as a chant in a town square can end up shaping a generation in a classroom if left unchecked.

Brookline and Newton felt different for me—personal in a way that Quincy or other towns never could. Brookline was where I grew up, where Jewish friends had shaped my childhood, where menorahs glowed in windows I'd passed as a boy. Newton was one of the most heavily Jewish communities in Massachusetts, a place where parents now whispered their worries about whether their children could even walk to school safely. To stand with flags in those towns carried a weight that was impossible to put into words. The activists who gathered there weren't just attacking "Israel." They were targeting the very heart of Jewish life in Massachusetts. Their chants of "from the river to the sea" weren't abstract slogans; they were threats aimed at neighbors, classmates, Holocaust survivors who still lived quietly in those very streets.

In Brookline, I remember one particular Saturday when they had planned a march for Palestine through the heart of town. It was supposed to be their show of force, their way of claiming Brookline's streets. But word spread quickly, and I pushed hard to rally the Jewish community. Calls, posts, messages—it became a groundswell. And when the day came, something extraordinary happened: they cancelled their march at the last moment. They saw the size and determination of the pro-Israel presence and thought better of parading their hate through the same streets where mezuzahs hung on so many doorposts. For once, their noise was silenced before it even began.

That same energy carried into a massive counter-protest against a cease-fire resolution that the Brookline Town Meeting was considering. The resolution, dressed up in the language of peace, was in reality nothing more than a one-sided condemnation of Israel. Over 200 of us showed up—Jews, allies, friends—packing the hall and the streets outside. Flags waved, voices rose, and the message was clear: Brookline would not bow to a false moral equivalence that erased Jewish suffering. The sheer size of our presence rattled them. For once, they weren't the majority. For once, they were forced to see that Jews and their allies were not going to roll over quietly.

Lexington carried a different symbolism. This was the town that prided itself on its Revolutionary heritage, where the first shots of American liberty were fired. To watch "Lexington for Palestine" stage their rallies there felt like a desecration of sacred ground. And it wasn't even homegrown. The group's loudest mouth wasn't from Lexington at all, but from Framingham—a man with open ties to the Iranian regime. The same regime that bankrolls Hamas, brutalizes its own people, and dreams of annihilating Israel. He came to Lexington not to honor its spirit of liberty, but to hijack it, to cloak imported hate in the borrowed language of revolution.

The local paper, the *Lexington Observer*, played its own insidious role. They didn't just report on the protests—they were embedded in them. Their coverage bent reality, casting the masked demonstrators as noble activists while ignoring the antisemitic chants and the threats hurled at Jewish residents. They erased the intimidation, scrubbed the ugliness, and presented propaganda as journalism. To read their accounts was to enter a parallel universe, one where hate masqueraded as justice and the people most at risk barely existed at all.

But the detail that always stood out most in Lexington—and in every town, really—was the masks. Again and again, I watched them march with keffiyehs pulled high, sunglasses hiding their eyes, hats or hoods shadowing their faces. If their cause was righteous, if their conviction was real, why hide? Why be afraid to show your face in the very community you claimed to be fighting for? The answer was obvious: because deep down, they knew. They knew their slogans were not calls for peace but calls for erasure. They knew ordinary people would recoil if they saw the true venom in their eyes. So they covered up, disguising cowardice as conviction.

I never wore a mask. I never hid my face. I stood with flags, visible and unflinching, across from their chants. In Brookline, Newton, and Lexington, I made the same choice: to stand openly where they concealed themselves, to embody the courage of presence where they relied on the comfort of anonymity. And in each of those places, the contrast was unmistakable.

Then came Beverly.

The local farmer's market seemed like the last place you'd expect confrontation. Rows of white tents lined the square, brimming with fresh strawberries, braided garlic, jars of honey, and hand-knit scarves. Parents sipped iced coffees while kids tugged at their sleeves, begging for cookies or balloons. It was small-town New England at its most charming, the kind of scene where neighbors greet each other by name and politics feels a world away.

But politics had invaded even here. Week after week, the pro-terror activists carved out a corner of the market, hiding their venom behind words like "justice" and "human rights." Their table was stacked with slickly designed pamphlets, all of them carrying the same message: Israel is evil, Jews are oppressors, Hamas is resistance. It was propaganda dressed up for polite company, slipped into the very space where families came to buy their food.

That Thursday afternoon, I arrived with a few friends. We weren't there to disrupt. No chants, no bullhorns. Just Israeli flags—bright, visible, undeniable. Silent symbols of resilience in a space where their lies had been allowed to spread unchecked.

At first, it seemed almost too ordinary. My friends stopped at a produce stand to chat with a garlic farmer. He was proud of his crop, explaining how he braided bulbs together for storage. His easy friendliness was the kind of interaction that made these markets worth visiting—neighbors connecting over something simple and good.

And then Alexandra appeared.

She froze the moment she spotted the flag, her whole body stiffening like she'd just seen a ghost. Her eyes narrowed, her jaw clenched, and within seconds the dam burst. She stormed toward us, her voice rising until it tore through the calm rhythm of the market.

"Get out of here! How dare you bring that flag here!"

Her hands trembled, her face flushed crimson, every muscle coiled with fury. It wasn't the kind of disagreement you see at political rallies. This was visceral, primal hatred, triggered by nothing more than the sight of blue and white cloth fluttering in the breeze.

I knew exactly what I had to do. In this fight, if it isn't on video, it didn't happen. I pulled out my phone, steadying my hand as best I could, and hit record.

That's when it happened—fast, deliberate. She lunged and slapped my hand, knocking the phone hard to the ground. A sharp crack echoed against the pavement. Gasps rippled through the crowd. The garlic farmer stepped back, eyes wide. Children stopped mid-stride, clutching their parents. For a split second, the market froze.

I bent down, picked up the phone, and kept filming. My pulse hammered in my ears, but my voice stayed calm. Assault—plain and simple.

Someone called the police. When the officers arrived, I showed them the footage. They watched it, nodded, and agreed that what she had done crossed the line. But then came the deflating caveat: Massachusetts law treats simple assault without serious injury as little more than a slap on the wrist. A summons, not an arrest.

At that moment, the message was clear. If you dare to stand for Israel in Massachusetts, don't expect the system to protect you. The rules bend when it's Jewish pride under attack.

And yet—even in that moment, I knew I had done the right thing. Because silence would have meant surrender. By pulling out my phone, by refusing to shrink back, by standing visibly with my flag, I forced the truth into daylight. Beverly's quiet farmer's market would never forget what it had seen: the mask of "human rights activism" ripped away, exposing raw, unfiltered hate.

Plymouth was different. Plymouth wasn't just another Massachusetts town—it was the birthplace of a nation, the soil where the Pilgrims landed, where Thanksgiving itself was rooted. It carried a weight of history that drew people from across the country, even the world. Families came to walk the waterfront, to stand at Plymouth Rock, to connect to something older and larger than themselves.

And yet, even here, the activists came. They showed up at the Rock, shouting slogans about "colonizers" and "genocide," as if desecrating a symbol cherished by generations of Americans was a legitimate form of protest. They harassed tourists—families with strollers, elderly couples taking photos, veterans visiting with their grandkids. Visitors expecting history and reverence were instead met with hostility. You could see it in their faces: bewilderment, anger, discomfort. Plymouth had welcomed them as guests, and they had spat on that hospitality.

It didn't stop there. That fall, they tried to target one of the most beloved traditions in New England: the Thanksgiving parade. Thousands turn out every year for it—bands marching, floats rolling, schoolkids waving to the crowd. It's wholesome, unapologetically American, the kind of event where you see veterans in uniform saluted as they pass by. And into that they tried to inject their poison, their chants and banners, hijacking a day meant for gratitude and unity.

But Plymouth wasn't having it. The locals, proud of their town and their traditions, refused to give them the reception they craved. Where in places like Cambridge or Lexington they found eager crowds, in Plymouth they found rejection. People turned their backs. Tourists booed. Residents told them to leave. And when we showed up with our flags, it was clear who the town stood with. The tourists gravitated toward us, not them. Kids pointed at our flags, parents nodded in approval, people came up to shake our hands.

That day, standing on the cobblestones with the American flag in one hand and the Israeli flag in the other, I realized this fight was never just about Israel. It was about the very idea of America. The same mobs that chanted for intifada were the ones trying to erase Plymouth Rock, trying to turn Thanksgiving into a day of shame instead of gratitude. They weren't just against the Jewish story—they were against the American story, too. Both, at their heart, are stories of survival, of faith, of carving meaning and freedom out of hardship.

Plymouth became a turning point for me. Until then, I had thought of my activism primarily as defending Israel and the Jewish people. But there, in the shadow of the Rock, I understood it was bigger than that. It was about defending the truth against those who wanted to rewrite history. It was about standing guard not only for Jerusalem, but for Plymouth, for Boston, for America itself. Because if they could erase Israel's right to exist, they could erase America's story, too.

And that realization gave me a new kind of fire. This wasn't only solidarity. This was patriotism. This was the defense of civilization itself.

Later that summer, Salem — a city forever haunted by the ghosts of its witch trials — became the stage for another showdown. And not just anywhere in Salem, but on the Salem Common itself. That green expanse, framed by old houses and iron fences, has seen centuries of gatherings, parades, and public reckonings. To me, the irony was staggering: the very ground where hysteria and mob justice once ruled was now being used as a stage for a new witch hunt — this time against Jews.

The activists had planned big. They staged a weekend-long encampment, dragging tents across the grass, banners unfurling in blood-red slogans: *"From the River to the Sea." "Resistance by Any Means Necessary."* Their chants cut through the air, angry and self-righteous. But beneath the theatrics, it was the same poison I had heard in Maynard, Newton, Brookline, and Quincy.

The whole operation came crashing down on something as basic as planning. They never secured a permit. Early that first morning, a porta-potty truck rumbled toward the Common, ready to set up. City officials intercepted it, and the verdict was blunt: *"No permit, no toilets."* The revolutionaries, so eager to scream about oppression, had skipped the simplest step of civic responsibility. No toilets meant no encampment, no matter how loud their slogans.

At the center was Jill, a local woman whose entire identity seemed bound to her marriage to a Palestinian man. She wielded that fact like a shield, as if proximity gave her the right to spew venom unchecked. Her sons, barely out of adolescence, mirrored her fury — stomping across the grass with signs smeared in red paint meant to mimic blood. They strutted and shouted, parroting slogans that were older and darker than they could ever fully grasp.

For a while, it seemed like the Common might tilt in their favor. But then Sunday came. And with it, something entirely different.

Rabbi Yossi arrived. He wasn't alone — he brought a small group from his community, men and women carrying flags, wearing kippahs, their presence a living answer to the hate that had tried to claim the Common. I joined them, and soon, what began as quiet solidarity grew into something stronger. Voices rose in song, Hebrew melodies filling the air, echoing against the old houses that ring the Common. And then we danced. Circles formed, flags waved, and joy itself became our protest.

The contrast couldn't have been sharper. On one side, clenched fists, scowls, chants of destruction. On the other, laughter, music, and light. People passing through the Common — families with iced coffees, couples with dogs, tourists tracing Salem's haunted history — stopped to watch. You could see it in their faces: the angry activists looked small, diminished, while we looked alive, unafraid, defiant in the truest sense.

That day on the Salem Common taught me something profound. Resistance doesn't always come with confrontation. Sometimes the greatest defiance is joy. To sing, to dance, to refuse to let hate steal the simple beauty of being alive — that is its own kind of victory.

The climax of the summer came in Cambridge. Harvard University. Move-in day.

The timing was deliberate — the coalition of communists, socialists, and pro-Hamas activists staged their encampment directly across from the gates of Harvard Yard, perfectly orchestrated for maximum visibility. Parents wheeled suitcases, freshmen lugged bedding and mini-fridges, and wide-eyed families took their first steps into what they thought would be a sanctuary of learning and opportunity. But instead of celebration, they were met with chants of *"Intifada, intifada!"* and *"From the river to the sea!"* echoing across the street like war cries.

We stood across from them with American and Israeli flags. No microphones, no slogans hurled back. Just presence. Just the simple act of showing that their narrative would not go unopposed.

Among the familiar faces was Jill — the same woman I had seen at Salem Common, still carrying herself with the righteousness of someone convinced that proximity to Palestinian suffering excused her venom. She stalked the edge of the encampment, glaring at us, egging on the younger activists around her, her voice carrying above the crowd like a conductor of rage. She had become a fixture at these spectacles, a self-anointed leader who mistook volume for conviction.

Then the Cambridge police arrived. Their posture was careful, cautious, as if they had been briefed to treat the encampment as delicate glass but us as a problem to be managed. One officer stepped forward.

"You need to move," he said to me.

"Why?" I asked, steadying my voice. "We're on a public sidewalk."

"You can't walk along the edge of the encampment," he replied.

I knew the answer before I asked, but I asked anyway: "That's unconstitutional. This is a public way. The First Amendment protects the right to walk, to hold a flag, to observe an event on public land. Do you know what the First Amendment says?"

Silence. The officer avoided my eyes. His hesitation wasn't ignorance alone; it was fear. Fear of enforcing the law evenly. Fear of applying the same standard to both sides. Fear of being accused of bias if he dared to uphold our rights.

That silence told me everything. Law enforcement, at least here, either didn't understand the law or had been cowed into abandoning it. In Cambridge — the city that likes to parade itself as a bastion of free speech, of academic inquiry, of intellectual courage — the Constitution was being bent in real time.

The irony was almost unbearable. At Harvard, the cradle of American higher education, parents and students walked through gates inscribed with mottos about truth and knowledge while the First Amendment was being trampled on the very street outside. The same amendment that guaranteed Jill and her comrades the right to spew hatred also guaranteed me the right to stand across from them with my flag. But in practice, the protections weren't equal. Their speech was celebrated, defended, coddled. Ours was treated as a nuisance, something to be pushed to the side.

That day crystallized something I had felt all summer but hadn't fully articulated: this wasn't just about Israel, or Jews, or the Middle East. It was about America. It was about whether the freedoms enshrined in the Constitution meant what they claimed to mean, or whether they were privileges doled out selectively to those who conformed to fashionable ideologies.

On move-in day, as parents hugged their children goodbye and snapped photos in front of ivy-covered gates, they may not have noticed the clash happening at the edge of the street. But I did. And I knew what I was witnessing wasn't just a protest. It was the slow erosion of civil liberties, playing out in real time, at the very doorstep of one of America's proudest institutions.

Boston has always been a city of history—Freedom Trail, Faneuil Hall, City Hall Plaza. But in the summer of 2024, it became a stage for something no history book could have prepared for: the Hostage Tunnel exhibit. A chilling, gut-wrenching reconstruction of the conditions inside Hamas tunnels, built to make people feel, even briefly, what it meant to be stolen from your home and dragged into Gaza.

I volunteered to help there for two days, and it wasn't just logistics. It was personal. I was asked to work with families of the hostages themselves, people whose lives had been shattered on October 7 and who now carried the burden of speaking for those who couldn't.

One of those families was that of Itay Chen, a young soldier whose absence left a hole so large you could feel it in the way his loved ones spoke his name. Standing beside his parents, watching them meet hundreds of strangers—dignitaries, students, ordinary Bostonians—I could see how every handshake carried weight, every photo was a cry for recognition. Their grief was an open wound, but they carried it with strength that bordered on superhuman.

I also worked closely with the sister and brother-in-law of Ohad Yahalomi, another hostage whose story tore through the plaza like a live wire. They weren't there to perform or to give speeches for the sake of politics. They were there because every hour, every minute, their loved one remained in captivity was another eternity of pain. And yet, they smiled for people. They answered questions. They relived the horror over and over, not because they wanted to, but because the world had to hear it.

My role was simple on paper: provide protection, make sure they felt safe as they engaged with the crowd. But in practice, it meant being a shield. I stood between them and anyone who lingered too long, who shouted too loudly, who tried to twist the narrative. I scanned the plaza constantly, reading body language the way I had in Iraq—watching for tension, for threat, for the sudden shift that could mean danger.

It wasn't combat, but it was a battlefield of another kind. These families were under siege—not by rockets or bullets, but by indifference, by propaganda, by the creeping sense that the world might forget their sons, daughters, brothers, sisters. And I knew in my bones that forgetting was as dangerous as any weapon.

For two days, I walked City Hall Plaza with them. I watched as politicians shook their hands and cameras flashed, as everyday people leaned in to say "we're with you," some with tears in their eyes. And every time I caught the sister of Ohad glance away, her jaw tightening as though holding back tears, I felt the urgency of it all over again. These weren't just symbols. These were families clinging to hope with both hands.

At night, after the plaza cleared, I would sit in my car and let it all hit me. I had stood guard in Bosnia, Kosovo, and Iraq. I had buried friends killed in battle. But this was different. This was grief in real time, stretched across days and months, lived by people who refused to let the world look away.

Those two days in Boston left an imprint on me. They reminded me why I show up, why I wave flags, why I refuse silence. Because behind every banner, every headline, every statistic, there are faces—parents, siblings, children—fighting not just for survival but for dignity.

By August, the fight was taking its toll. The drives were long—sometimes hours each way. The confrontations were draining, not just physically but spiritually. Standing in the sweltering summer heat with a flag in my hands, face-to-face with people screaming that Jews deserved to die, was the kind of exhaustion you couldn't just sleep off. It settled deep into your bones.

And it wasn't as if we were some massive movement. We weren't hundreds or thousands filling the streets. At best, on a strong day, there were maybe thirty or forty of us. On a lean day, twenty. A small cluster of determined souls holding Israeli and American flags against crowds that outnumbered us, against chants that tried to drown us out. We weren't a tidal wave; we were a sandbag wall, fragile but unyielding, holding back the flood as best we could.

And yet, even in that crucible, small moments of encouragement gave me the strength to keep showing up. A passerby leaned in close and whispered, "Thank you." A car horn blasting in solidarity as the driver waved an Israeli flag out the window. A grandmother who stopped, her voice trembling, told us she hadn't felt safe walking downtown until she saw us standing there. Those fleeting words, those nods, those honks—they mattered. They were reminders that this wasn't just threatened—and to stand anyway. We had already discovered the strength that comes not from crowds or slogans, but from presence, from simply refusing to yield the square. And we had already proven—to ourselves, to our enemies, and most importantly to the Jewish community—that silence was no longer an option.

That summer burned the hesitation out of me. By the time September arrived, there was no going back to quiet routines, no pretending this was someone else's fight. I didn't know the cost that was about to come. But I knew one thing with absolute clarity: when the test came, I would not be silent.about countering slogans in a town square. It was about presence. It was about sending a message to every Jew who walked by: you are not alone.

By the end of that summer, I realized what we were doing was less about persuasion and more about endurance. We weren't trying to change the minds of those screaming at us—they were too far gone. What we were doing was showing that someone was willing to say "Enough." That someone would plant their feet, raise a flag, and refuse to let hatred pass unchallenged.

The summer of 2024 was a crucible. We weren't just up against protesters; we were up against something larger—a system stacked against us. Biased institutions that bent rules to excuse antisemitism. Radicalized mobs that felt emboldened to threaten Jews in public. Cowardly officials who looked away. Police who too often shrugged, indifferent, afraid, or unwilling to act. Every confrontation felt like pushing against an entire structure of apathy and hostility.

And yet, through all of it, we came back. Week after week. Town after town. Between twenty and forty of us, armed with nothing but flags, conviction, and the refusal to stay silent. We bore witness to the growing tide of antisemitism masquerading as activism, and we marked a line in the sand: wherever it appeared, we would be there.

We didn't know what September would bring, or how profoundly it would upend my life. But looking back, I can see how that summer laid the groundwork for everything that followed. Each rally, each counter-protest, each flag held high in the face of hatred was more than an isolated moment—it was training, preparation, a proving ground. We had already drawn the battle lines.

We had already learned what it meant to be outnumbered, to be jeered, to be

Chapter 13:

September 12, 2024 — Flashpoint

Thursday, September 12, 2024, began like any other day. Nothing in those first few hours hinted at how profoundly the day would end. I woke up with the sun, the house quiet, the world outside calm. I brewed my coffee, the smell filling the kitchen as I leaned against the counter, letting the warmth of the mug soak into my hands. The air drifting in through the window was cool and clean, the first hints of autumn cutting through the leftover humidity of summer. Birds chattered. A neighbor's dog barked halfheartedly. For a while, life felt ordinary—comfortably, deceptively ordinary.

I moved through the familiar motions. Answered a few emails. Skimmed the news on my phone. Jotted notes about work I wanted to get done later. The headlines were predictable by then: the war in Israel grinding on, American universities descending further into radicalism, politicians fumbling through statements that sounded more like theater than leadership. It had all become background noise, like static you learned to live with. I sipped my coffee and exhaled, believing—naively—that this would be just another Thursday.

But beneath that calm exterior, something was shifting. And when I look back now, it feels almost like the stillness before a storm.

By the afternoon, I felt restless. Months of activism had taken their toll—weekend after weekend, town after town, standing against the tide. For a while, our numbers had been strong. Sometimes dozens of us would gather, flags waving in defiance, voices rising together. But as summer dragged on, reality set in. The numbers dwindled. Some weekends it was only a handful of us, sometimes just me. People burned out, and who could blame them? The drives were long. The confrontations were brutal. Standing for hours, listening to jeers, absorbing the venom—week after week—it wore people down.

And the confrontations weren't just words anymore. They were turning uglier, sharper. Cars swerved closer to us on the street. Protesters pushed boundaries, sometimes physically. The rage in their eyes told me it was only a matter of time before someone crossed a line. I could feel it in my gut: the atmosphere was changing. It wasn't sustainable to keep doing things the same way.

We needed to switch gears.

Up to that point, so much of what we had done was reactive—showing up wherever they showed up, countering their slogans, standing across from their rallies. It mattered, it showed resistance, but it was also draining. We were letting them dictate the terms of engagement. They chose the ground, and we followed. More and more, I could see the danger in that—not just strategically, but spiritually. We were caught in their negativity, forced to hold the line while they controlled the narrative.

I wanted something different. I wanted to seize the initiative. To create something uplifting, visible, undeniable. Something that wasn't about responding to hate but about radiating pride.

So we flipped the script.

Instead of countering, we would host our own. A solidarity standout, on our terms. No screaming matches, no being boxed into corners. Just us—joyful, visible, proud. Israeli flags waving against the sky, Hebrew music rising above the traffic, signs of love and resilience for Israel and the Jewish people. A statement of presence, not protest. A beacon, not a rebuttal.

I studied maps like I was planning an operation. I needed a location that amplified the message. Then I found it: the Harvard Street bridge over the Massachusetts Turnpike in Newton. The perfect vantage point. Thousands of cars passed beneath that bridge every rush hour, crawling through traffic with nothing to do but look up. Eastbound. Westbound. They'd all see us. And it wasn't just about commuters. The bridge connected to Washington Street, right in the heart of Newton's Jewish community. Families walked those sidewalks every day. Synagogues dotted the area. Holocaust survivors lived within blocks. This wasn't just about optics—it was about solidarity, planted firmly where it mattered most.

We set the time: 4:00 to 7:00 p.m. Peak rush hour. The moment when the most eyes would see us.

At the time, it felt like a turning point. What I didn't know was how quickly that turning point would turn into something much darker.

I arrived early. The late-day sun was still warm, painting the brick buildings of Newton in gold as it slanted toward the horizon. The air carried that unmistakable September sharpness, a hint of fall but still holding onto summer. We hauled our flags, posters, and a small speaker to the corner of Harvard and Washington. Within minutes, the ordinary bridge became something extraordinary.

Israeli songs filled the air. Some were upbeat and defiant, their rhythms daring anyone to silence them. Others were soulful, ancient melodies that seemed to carry centuries of longing. The music bounced off the pavement and brick, mingling with the hum of rush-hour traffic below. And then came the horns—at first tentative, then louder, more frequent.

Cars honked in rhythm as they passed under the bridge, drivers waving, passengers leaning out windows with thumbs up. It wasn't just noise. It was affirmation.

Families stopped to listen. Strangers I had never seen before mouthed the words "thank you." Others simply nodded, their eyes saying what words couldn't. For the first time in months, I felt it in my chest—not the tightness of confrontation, but the openness of joy.

It felt good.

It felt like home.

Looking around, I saw the people who had become my family—Jews and non-Jews alike, drawn together not by blood but by conviction. The energy was lighthearted, almost festive. For once, there was no mob across the street. No one chanted for intifada. No jeers, no threats. Just us. Proud. Unafraid. Radiant.

And as I stood there, flags snapping in the breeze, I couldn't help but think of the Rebbe's words: "In a hall of perfect darkness, even one small candle can banish the shadows." That's what we were doing—turning an ordinary bridge into a menorah, into a beacon. For all the months of standing toe-to-toe with hate, this was different. This was proactive. This was light.

I felt as if the Rebbe himself was whispering: Don't only fight darkness—create light. And here we were, doing exactly that.

I was riding high on that energy. For the first time in a long time, I felt balanced—like my activism and my spiritual searching were finally in sync. Just a week earlier, I had signed up for an online "Introduction to Judaism" course through the Lappin Foundation. Every Thursday night at 7:30, a small group of us logged in, curious and hungry to learn. That night would be only our second session. My plan was simple: hold the standout until sundown, then head home, log into the class, and continue this dual journey.

Action and reflection. Street and study hall. Activism and learning. Light in the public square, light in the quiet of study. It was the rhythm I had been searching for—activism with roots, resistance with meaning. For a moment, standing on that bridge as Israeli music soared into the September air, I felt like I had found it.

Around 6:20 p.m., a friend of mine decided it was time to head home. I walked her to her car, the two of us chatting about how well the standout had gone. There was laughter in her voice, the relief of having spent a few hours not in the shadow of confrontation but in the light of celebration. She popped her trunk, handed me a few bottles of water she had stashed in the back, and I carried them back toward the group, smiling as I passed them out. It felt like a small gesture of care to match the joy we had shared that evening.

That's when I heard it. Shouting.

At first, I barely registered. After months of activism, shouting had become the soundtrack of my weekends—the chants of "intifada," the cries of "river to the sea." Usually, it washed over me like static. But this voice was different. It wasn't the calculated call-and-response of a demonstration. It wasn't the smug sarcasm of a heckler. It was raw, jagged, unsteady. It was the sound of something unhinged.

I rounded the corner and saw a small cluster gathered near the edge of the bridge. Two Israeli women from our group stood there, their thick accents carrying even over the din. They were speaking with a young woman who had stopped to take pictures and ask questions, their conversation animated but not hostile. For a moment, it looked like the kind of spirited exchange I had seen dozens of times—passionate, even heated, but not dangerous.

And then I saw him.

Across the street, pacing like a caged animal, was a man I didn't recognize. Mid-20s, wiry frame, a blue shirt and black shorts clinging to him as though he'd been moving fast. A COVID-era mask pulled tight across his face, hiding everything but his eyes. And those eyes—wild, darting, brimming with rage—locked on us with a focus that made my chest tighten. His fists opened and closed at his sides, like he was rehearsing violence before committing it. His longish hair shook with every sharp pivot as he paced back and forth, unable to be still.

He wasn't part of the conversation. He wasn't even pretending to be. He stood outside of it, vibrating with something darker. Hatred wasn't new to me—I had been screamed at in Boston, surrounded in Quincy, cursed in Lexington, mocked in Plymouth. But this wasn't ordinary hate. This was something more primal. My gut recognized it before my brain did.

This was dangerous.

Every instinct I had from years of soldiering, from patrolling in Iraq and Kosovo, from reading body language that meant life or death, told me the same thing: this man was not here to debate. He was here to explode.

And so I stayed.

Others might have walked away, figuring it was just another heckler, another random passerby. But something in me—maybe call it an alpha instinct, maybe call it a guardian's burden—wouldn't let me leave. The two women didn't see him the way I did. They were still caught in conversation. The rest of the group was laughing, holding flags, and drinking water. But I felt it in my bones.

It was as if the Rebbe's teaching about the candle in the darkness echoed in my mind, only this time the darkness wasn't metaphorical. I wasn't just holding light; I was standing between it and something that threatened to snuff it out. I planted my feet, eyes locked on him, my body already bracing for what I knew was coming.

I didn't know his name, or what he would do, but I knew this much: I wasn't going anywhere.

He began yelling suddenly, his voice slicing through the music and the hum of traffic below. The two Israeli women froze, their eyes widening as his words poured out in a torrent of fury. He didn't just speak—he barked, each sentence punctuated by stabbing gestures of his hands. His arms whipped through the air, fingers pointed like daggers, his body coiled and uncoiled with every accusation.

I saw the fear flicker across the women's faces, and instinct took over. Calm but alert, I stepped forward, positioning myself between them and the storm gathering in front of us. My posture changed—shoulders squared, stance rooted, eyes locked on his. I didn't need to say much; my body spoke for me. "You'll go through me first," it said without words.

His rant turned to geography, though it was never really about geography. "The West Bank!" he spat, each syllable laced with venom. His arms carved wild arcs through the air, as if he could redraw the map with sheer force of will.

I met his fury with steady defiance. "That's Judea and Samaria," I said, my voice low but firm, a wall against his chaos. "It's Jewish land."

The words hit him like gasoline on a fire. His eyes—already wild—burned hotter. They darted left and right, then snapped back to mine with an intensity that made the hairs on my neck rise. His jaw clenched. His hands balled into fists so tight I could see his knuckles straining white against his skin. He lunged forward a half step, then pulled back, then forward again—an animal testing the limits of its cage.

He wasn't there for dialogue. He wasn't there for nuance or history. His whole presence radiated something deeper, darker. It wasn't about land or borders. It was about erasure—about shouting so loudly that the Jewish women behind me disappeared, about intimidating us into silence, about driving us off that corner.

And then—he snapped.

His pacing stopped. His body stiffened, and his rage erupted like a dam breaking. His voice rose into an unhinged scream, every muscle in his frame coiled to strike. The air seemed to shift, the joy of moments earlier replaced by a chilling certainty: this was no longer words. This was violence waiting to be unleashed.

Without warning, he lunged.

It was sudden, primal—a coiled spring snapping loose. He darted off the curb and into Washington Street, cars screeching, horns blaring as he weaved recklessly through oncoming traffic. Drivers swerved, brakes screamed, but he didn't care. His eyes were locked on us, and his body was a missile.

Adrenaline flooded me. My body knew what to do before my mind caught up. My right hand dropped instinctively to my belt, brushing the familiar grip of my Sig Sauer P365XL, the weapon I carried legally, trained to use, and prayed I would never need. My left hand shot out, palm forward, fingers spread like a command.

"STOP! GO BACK!" I roared, my voice carrying over the blare of horns and the pulse of Israeli music still spilling from our speaker.

For a split second, it worked. He froze just feet from me, the soles of his sneakers skidding slightly on the wet pavement. The crowd behind me went silent, watching, waiting. Our eyes locked, and the world seemed to narrow to just the two of us—predator and defender.

His eyes were bloodshot, his pupils darting, the whites laced with rage. He looked both exhausted and electric, like a man running on pure fury. He leaned forward, his chest heaving, spit flying from his lips as he screamed. Then, as if to punctuate his contempt, he hocked a glob of spit straight at me. It landed close, splattering near my shoes.

The crowd gasped. My stomach tightened, but I didn't flinch.

He raised his middle finger high, jabbing it toward me with violent force, his hand trembling with rage. It wasn't just a gesture—it was a promise of escalation. He stepped back, then forward again, like a man at war with his own restraint. The air was thick, charged, every muscle in my body coiled and ready for the next move.

Finally, he staggered backward, retreating across the street, his retreat more defiance than surrender. His voice cut through the din:

"You're packing?" he sneered, his mask slipping as he spat the words. "Really? You're packing?"

"Yes," I said, my voice steady, my stance unshaken.

"Why?" he demanded, his tone dripping with mockery but edged with fear.

I didn't hesitate. "Because of bitches like you."

Not polished. Not diplomatic. But in that moment, it was the pure truth. He represented exactly why I carried, why vigilance mattered, why silence was never an option.

And as he lingered across the street, still pacing, still glaring, still itching for another chance, I knew this wasn't over. His reluctance to retreat wasn't weakness—it was calculation. He was looking for an opening. And my instincts screamed: stay ready.

I backed away, every nerve on edge. My training told me what my gut already knew: this had crossed the line from angry words to imminent danger. His spit, his gestures, his refusal to leave—all of it had escalated. This wasn't just some heckler who would scream himself hoarse and walk away. This man was hunting for violence.

I kept my eyes on him, but my mind was already moving three steps ahead. We needed the police there—now. Not to intimidate him, not to punish him, but to create a barrier before something irreversible happened. My instincts screamed that this wasn't over. His pacing, his eyes, the way he leaned forward every time like he was testing his own restraint—it was all building to something.

I pulled out my phone, backing up slowly, never turning my body fully away from him. My thumb hovered, then tapped out 9-1-1. The screen glowed in the fading light as I lifted it toward my ear.

And that's when he saw it.

To him, the phone wasn't a lifeline. It was a challenge. A sign I was calling in authority, that his time was running out. His body stiffened, and then the decision came—violent, reckless, absolute.

He ran.

Not walked, not lunged—ran. Full tilt. His legs pumping, arms cutting through the air, rage propelling him forward. He bolted off the curb, darting between cars that swerved and honked, horns blaring in protest as he wove through the traffic like it wasn't even there.

I held the phone in one hand, dialing 911, but my entire world narrowed to him: a man consumed by fury, bearing down on me like a predator zeroing in on prey.

He closed the distance in seconds. And in that last split moment, as his feet left the ground and his body launched toward me like a missile, instinct kicked in one more time. I pivoted hard, turning my right side away, angling my body so that the pistol on my hip would be shielded, protected. I wasn't just guarding myself—I was guarding the weapon.

The last image burned into my mind before contact was his wild eyes and outstretched arms. Then, everything collapsed into impact.

He launched into me with the force of a battering ram, and I twisted instinctively, angling my right side away to protect my pistol. That adjustment saved my weapon—but it doomed my head.

The right side of my skull slammed into the pavement with a sickening crack. It wasn't just sound—it was sensation. A blunt, bone-deep reverberation that sent a shockwave down my spine. Stars burst across my vision, white and violent, blotting out the late-day sunlight.

The world spun. A sharp metallic taste filled my mouth. My ears rang with a piercing whine, so high-pitched it felt like it was drilling into my brain.

Pain flared down my arm as my wrist struck next, my watch shattering against the concrete. My sunglasses snapped, one lens skittering away across the sidewalk. My iPhone flew from my hand, landing hard a few feet away. The screen stayed lit, the open line to 911 still active, transmitting fifty-three seconds of chaos—every thud, every grunt, every ragged breath.

The fog hit instantly. A concussion fog. My brain staggered, struggling to process what had just happened. I knew where I was, but everything felt distant, muffled. Shapes blurred. Sounds warped. It was as though the world had been dunked underwater.

I tried to will my body into motion, but my limbs lagged, sluggish, disconnected from my intent. Instinct screamed at me: *stay awake, stay alert, don't let go.* Darkness licked at the edges of my vision, threatening to pull me under.

And through it all, I knew this wasn't over. He hadn't finished.

He was on me before I could even fully register the impact. The weight of his body pressed down, pinning me to the concrete. My skull throbbed from the blow, the fog still clouding my senses, but his arm wrapped tight around my neck snapped everything back into brutal clarity.

The air vanished. My throat constricted. His forearm dug into my windpipe like a steel bar, each squeeze compressing my airway tighter. My lungs screamed, my body bucked, and still he bore down, eyes blazing with feral rage.

Then I felt it—his left hand clawing at my belt. Fingers digging, scrabbling, pawing with manic desperation. He wasn't just holding me down. He was hunting. Hunting for the pistol strapped to my side.

That was the instant I knew. This wasn't a fight anymore. It wasn't about words, or politics, or protest. This was life or death. Mine. My friends'. The women were just a few feet away. Anyone within the range of hollow points if he got his hands on my Sig.

He wasn't trying to silence me. He was trying to arm himself.

And if he did, there would be bodies.

Time fractured into pieces. Seconds stretched like minutes. I'd felt this before—back in Iraq, back in Kosovo—that surreal edge where life hangs by a thread. The body knows what the mind can't articulate. Training kicks in. Instincts fire. Words vanish, replaced by raw calculation.

His fingers brushed the grip of my pistol. My chest convulsed, starved of air. My vision dimmed, dark shadows crowding the edges.

Not like this.

I twisted, every muscle screaming. My right side curled away, shielding the weapon, even as my hands fought to pry his grip from my throat. My body screamed in pain, but somewhere beneath the fog, the soldier in me roared awake.

I shoved, bucked, leveraged hips and shoulders. His arm slipped a fraction. My hand found the pistol. The texture of the grip was electric—familiar, grounding, life itself.

With everything left in me, I drew.

The barrel cleared the holster.

Bang!

The shot cracked through the Newton evening, louder than any honk, louder than the traffic below.

A split second. A single trigger pull. A choice made not in anger, not in panic, but in survival.

Chapter 14:
Terror in Newton — Blood on the Pavement

The shot was muffled—more a hard *pop* than a thunderous bang—because the barrel was close to his body. It wasn't the cinematic explosion of sound most people imagine. It was smaller, denser, but it tore through the silence all the same. For a heartbeat, the world froze around me.

I felt the recoil drive through my arms, into my shoulders, down my spine. My hands tightened instinctively, muscles contracting from years of training. The weight of the pistol was suddenly heavier, alive, vibrating with the aftershock of what I had just done.

The smell hit next—sharp, metallic, unmistakable. Burned gunpowder filled my nostrils, curling into the back of my throat. It mingled with the faint scent of car exhaust rising from the Pike below and the sweat on my own skin. That cocktail of smells—the battlefield, transplanted onto a Massachusetts sidewalk—made my stomach turn.

My ears rang, a shrill, piercing tone that seemed to come from inside my own head. The ambient noise of the world—horns honking, engines rumbling, music still faintly playing from the speaker—was drowned out. For a few seconds, I was deaf to everything but that ringing.

I became hyperaware of my body. My right side still throbbed from hitting the pavement earlier, my skull sore where it had smacked the concrete. My watch was cracked on my wrist, digging into the skin. My sunglasses were gone, my iPhone somewhere on the ground. I could feel my pulse pounding in my temples, the rush of blood fighting the fog of the concussion. My breathing was ragged, each inhale sharp, each exhale forced.

Around me, the world had shifted but I hadn't caught up to it yet. I could see mouths moving—friends, strangers, bystanders—but the words were fragments, muffled, drowned in that high-pitched whine. A woman gasped, another shouted something, a chorus of phones went up to capture the moment. But to me, it was all distant, like I was watching it happen through glass.

For years, I'd imagined what it would feel like to fire my weapon in defense on American soil. Not in uniform, not in Iraq or Bosnia or Kosovo—but here, at home. I had wondered if I would freeze, if I would hesitate. The answer was in my hands, in the acrid air, in the silence pressing down on me. I hadn't hesitated. I had done what had to be done.

And yet, even as I lay there—pistol still in hand, heart hammering, lungs burning—one thought kept pushing its way through the fog: *This isn't Baghdad. This is Newton. This is home.*

The normal world—New England commuters, brick sidewalks, kids walking home from after-school activities—had collided with the world I thought I had left behind. And I was standing in the middle, straddling both, trying to reconcile the impossible.

The fight was over. I could see it in his body, in the way his shoulders slumped and his eyes widened with that unmistakable look—the look of a man who has just been shot and knows it. He wasn't lunging anymore. The violence that had propelled him seconds earlier was gone, replaced by a dull awareness of his own broken body. His chest rose unevenly, his hand pressing instinctively to his side. That fight in him, the animal rage, had bled out with the bullet.

But others hadn't caught up to that truth yet. Two members of my group, adrenaline spiking from the chaos, charged toward him. Their fists were clenched, their faces twisted in fury. They were reacting like any human would after watching their friend nearly choked out on the pavement. They wanted to finish it.

"STOP!" I bellowed, my voice raw, commanding, cutting through the confusion like a whip crack. "Stop it now!"

They froze. My tone left no room for argument. Combat leadership never leaves you—it lives in the spine, in the voice, in the ability to take control of chaos before it spirals.

I forced my breathing steady, even as my head pounded from where it had slammed against the pavement. My right side still throbbed, my vision hazy from the concussion fog pressing in. None of that mattered. What mattered was discipline. Control. Law.

I set my pistol down deliberately on the ground, behind me, barrel angled away. "Secure it!" I barked, making sure someone nearby took responsibility. No mistakes. No accidents. The weapon was no longer part of the fight—it was evidence now.

Then I yelled into the air, voice booming: "Call 911!"

What I didn't realize at that moment was that my phone had already done the job for me. It was still lying on the concrete where it had skittered during the assault, screen glowing, the call connected. For fifty-three unbroken seconds, the dispatcher had heard it all: the grunts, the crash, the struggle for breath, the pop of the shot. Newton's emergency system already had the entire ordeal playing in their earpiece.

But I wasn't thinking about that. I was thinking like a soldier, like an EMT. The moment the fight ended, my body switched modes automatically: neutralize, then stabilize. Secure the scene. Control the group. Get help on the way. Protect everyone.

It was instinct. It was training. And it was the only thing keeping chaos from consuming the bridge.

The chaos hadn't even settled when instinct took over. First priority: secure the weapon. My pulse still thundered in my ears, but my hands moved with precision. I drew the slide back, cleared the chamber, dropped the magazine, and locked the pistol safe. Then, deliberately, I placed it on a guardrail, angled away from everyone, in plain sight.

I wanted no ambiguity when the police arrived. No confusion. No quick-draw assumptions about whether I was still a threat. I had been in enough combat zones, enough chaotic aftermaths, to know how fast misunderstandings could spiral. Everything about my body language, every movement, was calculated: calm, visible, controlled.

"Secure it," I told one of my people, motioning to the weapon. My voice was clipped, authoritative. They nodded and stepped in, guarding it until law enforcement would take over.

Only then did I turn my attention back to the man who had just tried to kill me. He was still conscious, but the fight in him was gone. His body told the story: shoulders slumped, face washed pale, lips trembling as shallow breaths rattled in his chest. I'd seen that look before — the look of someone who knew their body was failing, who felt the cold creep of shock setting in.

I approached with deliberate steps, eyes locked on his hands. He was dangerous still — maybe not with fists, but with words, with intent, with the hate that clung to him even as life seeped out.

"Lie flat," I commanded, voice firm. He obeyed, though his movements were weak and clumsy, the strength gone from his limbs.

I dropped to a knee, scanned the wound, and knew immediately what I was seeing. Blood seeped beneath his shirt in irregular waves, the telltale sign of internal collapse. Classic thoracic trauma. His eyes darted in panic, but his chest betrayed him, struggling to draw air.

"Take off your shirt," I ordered. His hands shook, but somehow managed. I pressed the fabric hard to the wound, locking my weight into it. My training had kicked in: neutralize, then stabilize.

That's when he opened his mouth. Broken words slipped between gasps: "Israel… colonizers… genocide…"

Even now. Even here.

Something snapped inside me. "Shut it," I barked, sharp and low. "Now's not the time. Focus on your breathing."

It was surreal — kneeling on Newton pavement, adrenaline still coursing, pressing first aid into the adomin of a man who had tried to take my life, who even in his own fading strength couldn't let go of his hate.

But that's what training does. It narrows chaos into steps. Secure the weapon. Control the scene. Save who can be saved — even when they'd never do the same for you.

Minutes later, the Newton Police screeched onto the scene, sirens slicing through the thick September air. Blue strobes lit up the brick buildings, the asphalt, the shocked faces of onlookers. The scene that had already felt surreal was now bathed in flashing chaos.

Officers poured out of cruisers with weapons drawn, their voices sharp and commanding. The words blurred together—"Hands up!" "Don't move!" "Step back!"—but I knew exactly what to do. My training had prepared me for this, even if I never imagined it would happen here, in suburban Massachusetts.

Slowly, deliberately, I rose to my feet. My palms faced outward, fingers spread wide. Every movement was measured, intentional. "I'm the shooter," I announced, clear and steady. My voice cut through the noise. "The gun is secure. The threat is down."

It wasn't bravado. It was discipline. I knew that hesitation, one wrong gesture, could mean another life lost—maybe mine. I had rehearsed this scenario in my mind countless times, not because I wanted it, but because years of military service had drilled into me a single truth: you prepare for the worst so that if it ever comes, you're not paralyzed by it.

The officers swarmed me in seconds. Rough hands seized my arms, spun me hard, pressed my chest against cold metal. Cuffs snapped shut around my wrists, biting into the skin. I felt the pat-down, the sweep for weapons, the clatter of gear against my belt. None of it surprised me. None of it offended me. They were doing their jobs, the same way I had done mine.

I didn't resist. I didn't argue. I didn't raise my voice. My only focus was ensuring the scene stayed safe for medics, that no one else would get hurt because of confusion or panic.

They shoved me into the back of a cruiser, the door slamming like a final punctuation mark. Through the plexiglass, I watched the world outside play out in fragments: medics kneeling over the attacker, their hands moving in quick, practiced rhythms; officers huddled around a bystander's phone, replaying the footage of the shooting; my friends clustered on the sidewalk, some crying, some shaking, all of them reeling.

And me? I sat alone in the hard plastic seat, wrists bound, my head throbbed from the impact on the pavement, the fog of concussion creeping in, but my thoughts were sharper than ever.

I had trained for this. I had war-gamed scenarios in my head a hundred times over: neutralize, secure, survive, comply. But training doesn't account for the silence that follows. For the look on your friends' faces. For the way your own voice echoes in your head when you say, *I'm the shooter.*

It felt like I was watching a movie of someone else's life—except it was mine. And nothing would ever be the same again.

The ride to the station was short, just a few minutes, but it felt like an eternity. The cruiser's engine hummed beneath me, the cuffs bit into my wrists, and the weight of what had just happened pressed down like a boulder. My head still throbbed from where it had smacked the pavement, and a metallic taste lingered in my mouth. The flashing lights outside painted the world in blue, flickering across the plexiglass like a warped movie reel.

When we pulled into the sally port, I felt it—the crash. Anyone who has seen combat knows the sequence: first the surge, then the dump. Adrenaline floods you during the fight, sharpens your senses, pushes you beyond fatigue or pain. But when the threat is neutralized and the body realizes it's safe, the system collapses. Shaking. Nausea. Cold sweat breaks out across the skin. A hollow exhaustion that feels like your bones have been drained.

"Wait," I told the officer, my voice steady but urgent. "Give me a second."

He paused. I leaned forward, breathing deep, forcing myself to keep control. The last thing I wanted was to vomit in the back of a cruiser or collapse on the station floor. I had fought too hard to survive. I wasn't going to let the aftermath make me look weak. After a few breaths, the world steadied. I nodded. "Okay. Let's go."

Inside, the procedure began. Photos. Fingerprints. The sterile rhythm of booking, impersonal and methodical. They didn't ask me much—just my name, date of birth, address. No one asked why I was there, no one asked what had happened. It was all by the book, as if the circumstances didn't matter, as if context was irrelevant.

Eventually, a sergeant approached, clipboard in hand. "Do you want to give a statement?" she asked.

I shook my head. "No. Not without an attorney." The words were automatic. Years of training, of briefings in the Army, of watching soldiers get chewed up by legal systems, had ingrained it in me: *lawyer up, no matter what.*

She nodded, jotting it down. Then her eyes narrowed slightly. "Are you physically hurt?"

"Yes," I admitted. There was no point in hiding it. My left pectoral—already torn twice before—burned with pain every time I breathed. My ribs felt bruised. My head still rang from slamming the concrete.

Medics were called. They loaded me into an ambulance and ferried me to Newton-Wellesley Hospital. Even there, the cuffs stayed on. Cold steel secured me to the bed as nurses cleaned the scrapes on my arms and the abrasions across my side. My watch was broken. My sunglasses shattered. My chest ached every time I moved.

Then came the State Police Crime Lab. They filed in with sterile precision, their presence colder than the handcuffs. Swabs scraped across my skin for gunshot residue. Cameras flashed as they photographed the bruises mottling my body. They bagged my clothing piece by piece—shirt, even my belt—treating every thread as evidence. I sat half-naked under harsh fluorescent lights, the cuffs rattling every time I shifted.

It was humiliating. Not because I didn't understand. I knew the procedure; I had seen it done countless times. But because I knew in my bones that I had done the right thing. I had acted to save lives—mine, my friends', strangers who had no idea how close they were to danger. And yet here I was, treated as though I were the criminal, stripped of dignity, reduced to a case number.

The irony gnawed at me. I had trained for moments like this my whole life—combat, chaos, the razor's edge of survival. I had survived the attack. I had neutralized the threat. I had even rendered aid. And now the system, the very one I thought I was protecting, chained me to a hospital bed as though I were the danger.

Back at the station, they led me down a hallway and into a holding cell. The door clanged shut behind me, and just like that, the world shrank. Eight feet by ten. Cold concrete walls that leached the warmth out of the air. A steel shelf jutting from the side, masquerading as a bed, with nothing but a scratchy wool-blend blanket folded at its edge. In the corner, a stainless steel toilet-sink combo, the kind that strips you of dignity just by existing.

Cameras stared from above, unblinking, recording every move. The hum of fluorescent lights buzzed overhead, harsh and unnatural. There was no window, no clock, no sense of time passing—just a sterile box that erased all markers of the outside world.

That was the worst of it: deprivation. Not of food, not of water—they gave me those in measured rations—but of time. Time disappeared. I had no idea if it was day or night, morning or evening. The rhythm of the world had been severed. In combat zones overseas, I had always known time—patrol briefings, radio checks, the rise and fall of the sun. Here, I had nothing. Just a blank wall and my own thoughts.

My mind spun. Replay after replay of the attack, the struggle, the shot. Questions clawed at me: *Had I done enough? Should I have seen it sooner? Should I have walked away?* Each time I pushed those thoughts down with the same answer: I had survived. My friends had survived. Innocent people on that bridge had survived. That had to mean something.

First, I called my daughter. My hands trembled as I held the receiver, though my voice came out steadier than I felt. She answered casually, with that light, distracted tone only a college student can have—half in her dorm, half scrolling her phone. She had no idea that her world, and mine, had just tilted.

"You need to come home," I said. My voice was calm, clipped, the way it always got when I needed her to know I was serious.

"Why?" she asked, the confusion sharp in her voice.

"I've been arrested."

There was a beat of silence, then laughter. She thought I was joking, pulling one of my dry, dark-humor stunts.

"Google 'Newton shooting,'" I told her, flat, no trace of irony.

The silence that followed stretched like a chasm. I could almost hear the weight land on her chest as she realized I wasn't kidding. I pictured her eyes widening, her stomach dropping, the dorm walls suddenly closing in. She didn't say much after that—there weren't words. But her silence told me she understood. My heart broke that this was how she found out that her father's name was now tied to headlines.

Next, I called USCCA, my self-defense insurance company. Training and instinct kicked in. I used the exact words they drilled into members during orientation and seminars: "I've been involved in a self-defense shooting." My voice sounded detached, almost mechanical, like I was reading from a script. I gave them the details they needed—location, my name, my contact. They were calm, professional, and reassuring. They promised legal support, and told me an attorney would be on the way. Hearing those words was like catching a rope in a storm.

When the calls were done, the cell swallowed me again. The adrenaline had drained out of my body, leaving behind a hollow exhaustion. My hands were still shaking, not from fear, but from the chemical crash that always comes after combat or crisis.

At some point, an officer slid food through the slot—a McDonald's bag, the standard station fare. Fries, a burger, a soda. The smell filled the cell, greasy and heavy, usually comforting but now revolting. I couldn't stomach a bite. My throat was tight, my mouth dry, my stomach churning. I stared at the bag for a long time, the golden arches mocking me from crumpled paper. Out there, people were driving through the same chain for dinner without a second thought. In here, under fluorescent lights and concrete walls, it was just another reminder of how far removed I already was from normal life.

Hours passed in a blur—pain radiating through my chest where I'd been struck, the dull ache of a concussion fogging my mind, the cold biting at my skin. Time didn't move forward; it pooled, stagnant, stretching into something unmeasurable.

I was alone with nothing but the echo of what had happened and the dread of what might come next.

Chapter 15:

Chains of Injustice — The Arraignment

Sometime later, the door to the holding area opened, and in walked Glenn with Yael at his side. Until that moment, I had felt like I was stranded in a storm with no compass, no lifeline. But when Glenn stepped in, the atmosphere shifted.

He introduced himself as my attorney, retained by friends who had moved quickly to secure representation. From the first moment, he radiated steadiness. Glenn wasn't just another lawyer—he was a trial lawyer with nearly thirty years of experience, someone who had stood in courtrooms across the country and fought battles far more complex than mine. He had cut his teeth as an Assistant U.S. Attorney for the District of Massachusetts, prosecuting everything from tax fraud to RICO cases. He handled complex grand jury investigations, lectured law enforcement and even professional athletes on compliance, and earned the Department of Justice's highest honors, including two Attorney General's Awards. He was a man prosecutors respected, because he had been one of them—and that gave him an edge few defense attorneys could claim.

Even his past before the law carried a certain weight. Glenn had once worked as a Marine Engineer, serving aboard merchant ships for the Department of Defense. He'd held a Chief Engineer's license, navigating vessels across oceans before he ever navigated the intricacies of federal court. That grit—born of responsibility, precision, and discipline—was still evident in how he carried himself.

He didn't waste time on small talk. He pulled out his phone and began documenting my injuries, photographing the bruises across my chest, the abrasions on my arms, the swelling along my temple. Every click of the camera was deliberate. Then he asked me to describe my condition, listening carefully as I laid out the pounding in my skull, the searing pain in my chest, the fog in my mind. His questions were sharp, precise, the questions of a man who knew exactly what details would matter later.

When he explained the charges, his voice was calm, steady—but the words hit me like artillery shells: assault and battery with a dangerous weapon. And worse still, a civil rights violation.

I almost laughed—not because it was funny, but because it was absurd beyond comprehension. I had fought for my life, prevented a terrorist from seizing my pistol, and now the Commonwealth of Massachusetts was branding me with the same charge used against racists who assault minorities in hate crimes. It was grotesque, a twisting of reality.

Glenn must have seen the disbelief written on my face. He didn't try to placate me. He didn't sugarcoat it. Instead, he went to work. He stepped out for a while, and when he returned, he brought news that landed like a breath of clean air in a suffocating room: "The civil rights charge has been dropped." Just like that, one mountain was removed from the pile. A sign, however small, that maybe reason still existed somewhere in the system.

But the reprieve was short. "Bail is being set at fifty thousand," he said flatly.

The number hit me in the gut. My whole body sagged under its weight. "I don't know how this works," I admitted, my voice low.

"How much can you come up with?" he asked, his gaze fixed on me.

I ran the mental math, fast. My savings, already battered by months of chaos. Maybe five grand, if I moved things around. "Five thousand," I said finally, hating how small it sounded.

He nodded, unflinching. "We'll work with that." His tone left no room for doubt. This was a man who had handled million-dollar fraud cases, who had trained thousands of federal agents, who had stood in front of juries with lives on the line. My case was serious—but to him, it was winnable. His confidence wasn't bluster; it was the calm of a man who had been here before and knew the path forward.

In that moment, humiliated, I felt the first flicker of hope. Whatever came next, I wasn't walking into it alone.

Later that afternoon came with the kind of indignity you don't forget. When it was time to head into court, there were no real clothes waiting for me, no chance to present myself as anything other than what they wanted me to be: a defendant stripped of dignity. Instead, I was shoved back into the same thin hospital Johnny I'd been wearing since the night before. The thing barely tied shut, exposing more than it covered, fabric gaping at the sides like some cruel joke.

It might have been bearable if I'd at least looked like myself, but the mirror had other ideas. My face was a map of fresh bruises and angry cuts, reminders of the violence that had landed me here. Walking into an arraignment like that — half-naked in a hospital gown, face marked and swollen — wasn't just uncomfortable, it was calculated humiliation.

They shackled my ankles, cuffed my wrists, and linked it all together with a chain. Each step rattled with a metallic reminder: I wasn't free. The officers marched me across the short distance between the police station and Newton District Court. The walk wasn't long, just a few dozen paces, but it felt like crossing continents. The September sun hit my skin, warm and steady, and I tilted my head back just enough to feel it. After nearly a day of fluorescent lights and concrete walls, even a few seconds of sunlight felt like a gift. I inhaled deeply, the crisp early fall air filling my lungs. For the first time since the shooting, I felt human again.

Then the doors closed behind me, and I was back underground, funneled into another holding cell. Same concrete, same steel, same waiting.

And then came the final insult. I was marched up a set of stairs and locked into a glass box that separated me from the rest of the courtroom. Elevated, exposed, on display like some dangerous animal at the zoo. The prosecution sat polished in their suits and ties, looking every bit the part of authority and order, while I stood there in paper-thin fabric and visible wounds, stripped of dignity, identity, and humanity.

I wasn't standing before the court as a professional man fighting for his freedom. I was being paraded as a broken patient, a spectacle behind glass. The message was unmistakable: I wasn't strong or capable. I was to look beaten, vulnerable, and defeated — and that's exactly how I felt with every step toward the courtroom doors.

I braced myself for emptiness. Maybe a lawyer or two. Maybe my daughter, if she could get there in time. But when I entered, the sight stopped me cold. The gallery was packed. Shoulder to shoulder. Friends who had known me for years. Allies from the activism circles I'd stood with in Maynard, Brookline, and Newton. And people I didn't even recognize—strangers who had only read the headlines but had still come to show support.

It was overwhelming. I wanted to look at them, to nod, to acknowledge what their presence meant. But I couldn't. I knew if I met a single pair of eyes, the dam would break. The tears would come, and I couldn't afford that. Not here. Not now. I had to stay composed—for my daughter, for my mother, for myself.

The arraignment itself barely registered. Words floated by—"charges," "conditions," "bail set at $5,000 cash." GPS monitoring. Standard pretrial restrictions. It was over in minutes, but the weight of it pressed down all the same.

Afterward, Glenn leaned close, his voice steady. "Your friends raised the money on the courthouse steps," he told me. "In minutes."

I swallowed hard, throat tight. I'd faced war zones, mortar fire, violent mobs—but nothing compared to the humility of that moment. In my darkest hour, my people had shown up. Not just in words, not just online, but in flesh and blood, standing outside with cash in hand to set me free.

Gratitude washed over me like a tide. Shock, too. I had never asked for this kind of loyalty. And yet, there it was. Proof that when you stand for others, sometimes—when you need it most—they stand for you.

I was released under strict conditions. One of them: stay out of Newton. The irony cut deep. I had been attacked in Newton, nearly killed in Newton—and now, by order of the court, I was the one forbidden from setting foot there. Justice turned on its head.

Before I left, probation strapped a GPS monitor to my ankle. Cold plastic and steel, tight against the skin, a constant reminder that my freedom was conditional. I signed stacks of release paperwork with trembling hands. My shoes were returned in a plastic bag, laces removed, as if I were still a threat to tie them into a weapon. Every step was heavy with humiliation.

And then the doors opened.

I had braced for silence, but what met me was a wall of chaos. Cameras, microphones, reporters shouting questions over one another. Flashbulbs popped, voices called my name, headlines were already being written before I had taken two steps. It felt like walking into a battlefield, except this time the ammunition was words and lenses.

As I prepared to walk out of the court house doors, my friends stepped forward. They formed a shield around me—human armor, shoulder to shoulder—escorting me through the gauntlet. These weren't lawyers paid to protect me. These were people who loved me, who believed in me, who weren't afraid to take the blows of the press just to get me to safety. The sight of them—calm, defiant, unyielding—was almost too much to process.

I kept my head down. Said nothing. Not one word. Anything I said would be twisted, weaponized, plastered across headlines. Silence was my only defense. My friends guided me to the waiting car as the media swarmed, questions snapping like gunfire. It was only when the door shut and the world's noise dulled that I exhaled.

Yael was behind the wheel. She didn't say much, just drove steady, carrying me back to Framingham as if it were the most natural thing in the world. In the passenger seat, I called the Framingham police to inform them I was alomost home. I knew the police would request that my firearms be secured. Sure enough, not long after, three officers showed up, carrying printouts—Massachusetts' infamous "non-registry registry." Every weapon I had ever purchased was listed in black and white: rifles, pistols, ammunition. Piece by piece, they collected them all.

And then the house was quiet. Just me and my daughter. The adrenaline was gone. The noise of the courthouse, the flash of cameras, the cold metal of shackles—all of it had faded. What remained was the simple, fragile reality of sitting across from my child, knowing everything had changed.

We hugged hard, tighter than we had in years, like we were trying to fuse the broken pieces of our world back together. She cried. I did too. There was no stopping it. The dam had cracked, and everything we'd both been holding inside came pouring out.

She had already seen the video. Leaked to *The Daily Wire*, bouncing across social media, dissected by strangers who didn't know me, didn't know her, didn't know the truth. My daughter, who had grown up with me as her protector, her constant, was now watching me fight for my life on a sidewalk, framed in shaky cell phone footage. It was trauma on repeat, impossible to unsee.

And it wasn't just the horror of the attack. She was studying criminal justice, building a career on the very principles now turning against me. She understood in her bones what most people never fully grasp: the system doesn't always reward the righteous. Innocence doesn't guarantee protection. Self-defense doesn't guarantee freedom. She knew it, academically. But now she was living it, personally—through her father.

I wanted so badly to tell her it would all be okay, to give her the certainty that fathers are supposed to give their daughters. But I couldn't. The words caught in my throat. I didn't know if they would be true. And lying to her was something I had never done, something I refused to do now.

So instead, I did the only thing I could: I held her. I let her cry into my shoulder, let her grief soak into my shirt, let the moment last as long as it needed to. And in that silence, I prayed—not out loud, not with words, but deep in my chest, a raw plea for strength. For her, for me, for whatever came next.

Eventually, I pulled back, wiped her tears with my thumb, and kissed her forehead. Then, with a heart heavier than I've ever known, I picked up the phone. It was time to call my mom.

Chapter 16:

Shackled at Home — Prison Without Bars

The conditions of my release were made crystal clear the moment I stood in front of the judge. Each one landed like a hammer, stripping away pieces of the life I had known. No weapons of any kind—none—despite the fact that I had lawfully defended myself from a terrorist attack. Years of training, careful responsibility, and a spotless record meant nothing now. The Commonwealth wasn't interested in context. They wanted control.

I was barred from entering the town of Newton entirely, the same place where I had nearly been killed. The irony cut deep: attacked in Newton, arrested in Newton, and now exiled from Newton—as though I were the criminal, as though the danger had been me, not the man who lunged across a street to end my life. I was told I could pass through only if traveling on a major highway, but never to stop, never to set foot on its streets again.

Then came the no-contact order. I was forbidden from contacting my attacker in any way—not that I had any desire to. The very thought of being tethered legally to the man who tried to kill me felt like salt in an open wound. He had invaded my life with fists and fury, and now the court system had codified that invasion in black and white. His name was written into the restrictions that governed my every move.

But the harshest blow—the one that turned my house into a prison—was the curfew. From 7 p.m. to 6 a.m. on weekdays, I was forbidden from leaving my home. On weekends, the chains tightened even more: from Friday night until Monday morning, I was locked down completely. No dinners out. No Shabbat services. No late-night walks to clear my head. No spontaneous joy. The world shrank to four walls and a ceiling, and the outside might as well have been another country.

And then came the final indignity: the ankle monitor. A clunky, black shackle strapped to my leg, buzzing and digging into my skin. Every step I took reminded me that I was no longer a man presumed innocent. I had not been convicted of a crime, but the device made sure I felt like a convict every waking hour. I had traded one set of shackles for another—steel for plastic, a cell for my own living room.

The judge had not sentenced me to prison, but the Commonwealth had done something just as effective. They had made my home into one. My freedom was gone, my dignity under siege, and the message was unmistakable: you may have survived the terrorist attack, but you will not escape the system.

The ankle monitor wasn't just humiliating—it became its own form of harassment. At first, I told myself I could adapt. Like breaking in a stiff pair of boots, I figured it would be uncomfortable at first, but eventually, I'd stop noticing it. I was wrong.

The device had a mind of its own. It wasn't just clunky and obvious; it was inaccurate. In the dead of night, at two or three in the morning, I'd be startled awake by the vibration of my phone. On the line was a voice from the GPS monitoring center demanding to know why I had "left my residence." My heart would hammer as I explained, half-asleep, that I was in bed, staring at the ceiling. Sometimes I even had to get up in the middle of the night and walk around outside until the GPS stabilized. Still, the tone on the other end was always the same: guilty until proven innocent.

The glitches kept coming. Alerts buzzed while I was cooking in the kitchen. They went off while I sat on the couch, TV remote in hand. Once, I was in the shower, steam fogging the bathroom mirror, when the calls came through. By the time I got out, I had three missed calls, each accusing me of fleeing my own home. I'd call back, exasperated, dripping water onto the floor, trying to explain the absurdity of being "on the run" while standing barefoot in my own bathroom.

Each time, I felt less like a man and more like an inmate in some invisible prison where technology ruled over truth. A glitch in their system carried more weight than my word, more authority than my integrity. There was no space for common sense, no recognition of who I was or what I had endured.

What wore me down most wasn't the ankle chafing my skin, or the humiliation of explaining it to neighbors—it was the constant sense of being hunted. The buzzing alerts were like a predator's footsteps, reminding me I wasn't free, that someone, somewhere, was always watching and waiting for me to slip up. I couldn't relax, not even in my own living room. Sleep became fractured, restless. Every vibration jolted me awake, my body bracing for accusation.And through it all, my daughter watched. She tried to be brave, but I saw the shadow in her eyes when she looked at the black plastic cuff clamped to my ankle. She had grown up knowing me as a soldier, a protector, a man of discipline and strength. Now, she saw me hobbling around the house with a device meant for criminals. To her, I wasn't just her dad anymore—I looked like someone serving a sentence. That was the part I hated most.

The GPS wasn't just a monitor. It was a scarlet letter. A reminder that even after surviving an attack, even after defending myself and others, the system saw me as the problem. And it will never let me forget it.

The financial hit came like a freight train. I'd barely wrapped my head around the GPS monitor, the curfew, and the humiliation of being treated like a criminal when the next blow landed.

I've worked my entire life. From the time I was a teenager, I always had a job. I'd gone from menial work in Brookline to the Army, to professional civilian careers. There was never a season of my life where I wasn't earning my keep. It wasn't just about money—it was about dignity. Work was how I measured myself. It was how I kept food on the table, how I modeled responsibility for my daughter, how I kept my own sense of order intact. I had always been a provider. Always.

So when I picked up the phone to call my employer, I already knew it would be a difficult conversation. I braced for bad news. But what I heard was worse than anything I could have prepared for. One of our biggest clients, National Grid, didn't want me on their projects anymore. Not because my work was lacking. Not because I had failed a test, missed a deadline, or cut a corner. Simply because of the "incident."

A man had tried to kill me, and somehow, I was the liability.

I hung up the phone and sat in silence. The room felt colder, smaller, as if the walls were closing in. My chest ached—not from the bruises of the attack, but from the injustice. I had spent my whole life working, never taking handouts, never letting myself or my family slip. And in one moment, it was stripped from me. No trial. No verdict. Just erased, blacklisted, as though my willingness to defend myself and others had made me unfit for honest work.

The hit wasn't just financial—it was existential. Work has always been part of my identity: the soldier, the employee, the professional, the provider. And now, I was being told I couldn't provide anymore. I was being told I was radioactive, untouchable.

Explaining it to my daughter was worse than hearing it myself. She asked the question no parent ever wants to hear: *"Are we going to be okay? Can we still pay for food and bills?"* Her voice was steady, but her eyes gave her away—she was scared.

I told her yes, of course we'd be okay. Because that's what a father does. He steadies the ship, even in a storm. But deep down, I wasn't sure. The math was brutal. Bills didn't stop coming just because life exploded. Groceries didn't stop costing money just because a court slapped an ankle monitor on me. And I had never, in my entire life, been without a job.

Now, for the first time, I was staring at that void—and it terrified me.

It felt like the system wasn't just punishing me—it was dismantling me. Piece by piece, the life I had built was being stripped away, until all that remained was a shadow of the man I had been.

The first piece to go was my freedom. I had survived a terrorist attack, fought through the fog of a concussion, and protected lives, only to find myself chained by a GPS monitor. I couldn't leave my home after dark. I couldn't go to synagogue. I couldn't even take a walk on a Sunday morning. My world shrank to four walls and a schedule dictated by the Commonwealth, as if I were the criminal.

Then came dignity. Every false alert from the ankle monitor, every phone call at 3 a.m. accusing me of fleeing when I was lying in my own bed, chipped away at my humanity. I wasn't a father, a veteran, or a man with a lifetime of service behind me—I was an inmate on borrowed time, treated like a fugitive for living in my own home.

And then, work. Losing my job wasn't just a financial blow—it was an assault on my identity. I had *always* worked. Through deployments, through hardship, through single parenthood, I had never once been idle.

But now, because I had survived and defended myself, I was radioactive. National Grid dropped me. My livelihood evaporated. My daughter looked at me with questions in her eyes I couldn't answer. For the first time in my life, I had no paycheck coming, no clear way to provide.

Piece by piece, it was stripped away—freedom, dignity, work. Each loss carved out another part of me until I felt hunted not only by the mobs in the street, but by the very system that was supposed to protect me. It wasn't just injustice—it was disassembly. A slow, methodical unmaking of the man I had spent a lifetime becoming.

If the Commonwealth tried to cut me off from the world, my friends and allies made sure I never disappeared into that isolation. They showed up—not just once, not just in the big moments, but day after day in the small, quiet ways that keep a man from breaking.

Hot meals arrived at my door with little notes tucked into foil or taped to Tupperware: *We're with you. Stay strong. Am Yisrael Chai.* Some came from people I had known for years, others from folks I had only recently met on the sidewalks of Maynard, Newton, or Brookline. Each plate of food carried more than calories—it carried defiance against the narrative that I was alone.

My phone never stopped buzzing. Text messages filled the screen: prayers, words of encouragement, even dumb jokes meant to pull a laugh out of me when I couldn't find one myself. Calls came at all hours, especially late at night when the ankle monitor pressed hardest on my spirit. Sometimes it was just a voice on the other end saying, "I just wanted to check in." Other times it was silence, a friend sitting with me over the line so I didn't feel caged in my own house.

And then there was the rally. At the very site of the attack, people gathered—not just to protest what had happened, but to reclaim the ground where my life had nearly ended. Flags waved, songs were sung, and voices rose in unity. Dozens came—Jews and non-Jews, young and old. They weren't there for themselves. They were there for me, to remind me that the bridge where I had nearly been killed was not just a place of trauma. It was a place where the community stood up, where light pushed back against darkness.

I can't name everyone who cooked, who texted, who stood in the rain holding a flag. They know who they are. But what I can say is this: without them, the isolation might have broken me. With them, I endured. Every meal, every message, every rally was a reminder that while the Commonwealth might have shackled my ankle, it hadn't shackled my spirit. My people wouldn't let it.

My legal team moved fast. Glenn understood that time was both our enemy and our ally. Every day that passed, the media spun its stories, the DA's office plotted its strategy, and the public made judgments before a single piece of evidence was presented. We couldn't afford to waste a second.

Meeting after meeting, he walked me through the labyrinth of the case—witness statements, video footage, dispatch recordings, forensic reports. We built the defense brick by brick, not with theatrics but with cold, undeniable truth. And the truth was simple: I hadn't broken a single law. I had done exactly what my training had prepared me for. I had acted with discipline, not malice. I had neutralized a deadly threat and protected lives.

From the beginning, I made one thing clear to Glenn and to anyone who asked: there would be no plea deal. I would not plead guilty to something I had not done. To do so would be to betray myself, my daughter, my friends, and the principles that had guided me my entire life. Marian Ryan might have thought she had her next easy headline, another political scalp to wave around, but I wasn't going to hand her that victory. I'd been through battles far worse than this one, and I was prepared to fight to the end.

But even as we built the case, the daily torment of the GPS monitor wore me down. The false alerts, the middle-of-the-night phone calls, the constant presumption of guilt—it was harassment by machine. I could feel it digging into me, not just physically but mentally, a reminder every minute of every day that the system wasn't interested in justice, only control.

By early October, after weeks of sleepless nights and countless disruptions, Glenn had had enough. He filed a petition to have the device removed. This wasn't just about comfort—it was about exposing how broken the system was, how unreliable the so-called safeguards had become.

And so, the next battle was set. On October 7—one year to the day after the Hamas massacre that had lit this fire inside me—I would stand before a judge once again. This time, not just to defend myself, but to challenge a system that had shackled me in the name of justice. The symbolism wasn't lost on me. October 7 had changed my life once already. Now, it was about to change again.

The hearing was set for October 7. The date carried its own heavy symbolism—exactly one year since Hamas had unleashed its massacre in Israel, the day that had changed the trajectory of my life. And now, here I was, standing before the Commonwealth of Massachusetts, fighting for my own freedom on that very anniversary.

It wasn't even in a courtroom. Appropriately, it was held over Zoom—one of those lingering quirks of the post-pandemic world, where something as consequential as liberty could hinge on the quality of an internet connection. I sat on my couch in a collared shirt, laptop propped up, the ankle monitor buzzing faintly at my leg as if mocking me one last time.

As the session began, my chest tightened. Would the judge see the truth? Or would this be another round of humiliation, another exercise in politics over justice? For weeks, the device had been my jailer. Every false alarm, every midnight phone call had chipped away at my sanity. And now, it all came down to this.

But as soon as the assistant district attorney began to speak, my anxiety gave way to something else: confidence. He was unprepared, fumbling for words, clearly out of his depth. When asked to justify why I needed to remain shackled to a faulty GPS monitor, he stammered. When pressed on why I should be barred entirely from Newton—a town where I had been the victim, not the aggressor—he shrugged. At one point, red-faced and flustered, he asked for a fifteen-minute recess to "consult." The break dragged on awkwardly, and when he finally returned, he still had no answers.

At that moment, the mask slipped. The case against me wasn't about justice, or safety, or law. It was about optics, headlines, and political calculations. I wasn't being treated like a citizen. I was being treated like a scapegoat. But the judge saw through it.

When the decision came down, it felt like oxygen rushing back into my lungs: our petition was granted. The GPS monitor was to be removed immediately.

I didn't waste a second. I showered, put on decent clothes, and drove straight to Newton District Court, heart pounding with anticipation. Walking into that courthouse, I knew something was about to change. The clerk led me into a side room where a probation officer was waiting.

The removal process itself was simple, almost anticlimactic—a few clicks on a keyboard, a twist of a key, the sharp snap of plastic unfastening from my ankle. But for me, it was strangely emotional. For nearly a month, this device had dug into my skin, left bruises, tracked my every move, and accused me of violations I hadn't committed. It had been my shackle, a constant reminder that the state considered me guilty until proven innocent. Watching it come off was like surfacing from underwater after holding my breath too long.

I recorded the moment on video, holding the clunky black device in my hand before setting it on the table. I sent the clip to a few close friends who had been with me since the beginning. Their replies came quickly—cheers, blessings, messages of relief. It wasn't just the end of a restriction. It was a symbol.

The state had tried to shackle me, to humiliate me, to break me piece by piece. But on October 7, of all days, their attempt failed. On the very anniversary of the darkest day for the Jewish people in this century, I tasted freedom again.

And I knew, deep in my bones, that the fight was far from over. But now, I would face it unshackled.

That same night, there was a vigil on Boston Common to mark the one-year anniversary of the October 7th terrorist attacks on Israel. The irony wasn't lost on me: in the morning, I had walked into a hearing shackled by the Commonwealth. By evening, I was walking freely into a sea of Jewish pride and resilience.

I hadn't told anyone I was coming. Part of me wanted it that way. I wanted to appear unannounced, to step into the circle not as someone weighed down by restrictions but as a man who had fought, endured, and reclaimed his place. It wasn't about spectacle—it was about presence. I wanted my people to see me there, unshackled, standing tall.

By the time I arrived, the rally was already underway. The Common glowed with candlelight, flames flickering in the October breeze. Israeli flags rippled against the night sky, their blues and whites luminous under the streetlights. Hand-painted signs bobbed above the crowd: *Never Again Is Now. Bring Them Home.* The air carried the mixture of grief and defiance that has become the heartbeat of Jewish gatherings since October 7.

At first, I lingered on the fringes, just taking it in. The prayers, the songs, the solemn silence between speakers—it washed over me like a tide. For weeks, I had been trapped in my home, treated like a criminal, watching the world move on without me. Now, I was standing in the middle of Boston, surrounded by hundreds of people holding candles and flags, all declaring with one voice that the Jewish people endure.

And then it happened. Word spread through the crowd: *He's here.* Faces turned, eyes widened, and one by one, friends made their way toward me. There were hugs, fierce and unreserved. There were tears, hot and cathartic. And there was laughter too—the kind that comes when a burden suddenly feels lighter. For the first time in weeks, I wasn't "the defendant" or "the man under house arrest." I was just me again—a brother among his people.

We sang *Am Yisrael Chai,* our voices lifting above the hum of the city. We prayed for the hostages still in Gaza, for the soldiers fighting on the frontlines, for the families who would forever carry loss. We mourned, yes—but we also celebrated survival. For a few hours that night, the weight I had been carrying slipped away. What replaced it was something stronger: joy. Not the fragile joy of denial, but the fierce joy of standing tall in the face of hate.

As the crowd thinned and candles burned low, I stood near the vigil, reluctant to leave. That's when a woman approached quietly, almost hesitantly. She introduced herself as Kimberly Bookman from Channel 7 News. Her voice was calm, her demeanor respectful, without the sharp edges I had come to expect from reporters. She handed me her card, saying softly, "Whenever you're ready to speak, I'd be happy to share your story."

It caught me off guard. After weeks of biased headlines and sensational coverage, this simple gesture felt like a lifeline. For once, a journalist wasn't looking for a soundbite to twist. She was offering a platform, a chance to tell the truth. It was small, but it meant everything.

Driving home later that night, candlelight still flickering in my memory, I couldn't shake the contrast. The day had begun in confinement, shackled and surveilled. It had ended in freedom, surrounded by song, laughter, and light. The state had tried to define me by restriction. But my people had reminded me of who I really was.

On the anniversary of one of the darkest days in Jewish history, I found joy—not in forgetting the horror, but in standing tall against it. That night on Boston Common, I felt something I hadn't felt in a long time: hope.

What do you do when your character is dragged through the mud, when your name is smeared before a jury is ever seated? What do you do when you're punished not for a crime, but for surviving one?

You fight. You speak. You refuse to go quietly.

This chapter of my life was soaked in bitterness, but it was also lit with unexpected beauty. The bitter taste of injustice was sharp and unrelenting—cold cells, ankle shackles, headlines written by people who didn't care about the truth. But alongside it stood the sweet memory of candles flickering in the Boston wind, of voices singing *Am Yisrael Chai* under the stars, of friends who stood shoulder to shoulder with me when the world wanted me silenced.

Healing, I've learned, doesn't come from prosecutors or politicians. It doesn't come from newspapers chasing clicks or judges afraid of optics. Healing comes from people—the ones who look you dead in the eye and say, *We believe you. We're with you. Keep going.*

Yes, I still worry about money, about work, about the endless grind of legal battles yet to be fought. The system tried to strip me bare—piece by piece, day by day—but it never broke me. And it never will.

Because I am not alone. And I am far from done. The people who hate Israel, who hate Jews, who hate anyone who dares to stand for truth—they want silence. What they've gotten instead is me, louder, stronger, and more determined than ever.

The fight is far from over. And I'm not backing down.

Chapter 17:

Between Rockets and Roots — Israel Under Fire

From October until now, the only restriction on my freedom of movement was to stay away from my attacker. My passport was never taken. I was allowed to travel. I didn't even have to notify anyone of my plans, which struck me as one of the many absurd ironies of this ordeal. The Commonwealth had shackled me with an ankle monitor, locked me into curfews, and barred me from walking freely in my own town—but if I wanted to leave the country entirely? Not a single word of protest. For a month, they treated me like a prisoner inside my own home, but when it came to crossing an ocean, they had nothing to say.

It was a Friday night in late March when everything shifted. I was on the phone with a friend, someone I had stood beside at rallies and vigils, someone who had seen the best and worst of this fight alongside me. She mentioned casually, almost in passing, that she was flying to Israel at the end of April. Her words landed differently with me than she probably intended. I asked a few questions—what airline, which airport, what times—trying to sound casual. But already my heart was racing.

As she answered, I pulled open my laptop, fingers flying. Prices weren't impossible. The logistics weren't unmanageable. For the first time in months, something real and good was within reach—something restorative, something more than survival. I sat silent for a while, running the math in my head, weighing the risks, feeling the anticipation rise like a tide. Then, with a grin in my voice I couldn't contain, I interrupted her:

"Great. I'm on the same flight as you."

She laughed, realizing I had just bulldozed my way into her trip. But she didn't mind. Over the past year, we had been through much together for this to feel like an intrusion. If anything, it was natural. She'd been to Israel before; she knew the rhythm, the streets, the pulse of the land. Having her there made the leap feel less intimidating. As it turned out, we would end up sharing an Airbnb. She became my guide. I became her unexpected travel companion. Together, we were about to write a chapter that would mean more to me than I could have ever imagined.

The night before departure, I packed slowly, deliberately. It wasn't just shirts and pants I was folding into a suitcase—it was the weight of everything I had endured over the past year. The cold concrete of the cell. The humiliation of the ankle monitor. The endless false alarms, the media circus, the courtrooms. Every item I placed in that bag felt like a declaration: I'm still here. I'm going. I'm free enough to go.

When morning came, Logan Airport looked the same as it always did—crowded, fluorescent, humming with travelers. But to me, it felt transformed. My world for months had been measured in blocks and curfews. Now, holding a boarding pass to Tel Aviv, my radius of movement stretched across an ocean. The TSA checkpoint was perfunctory, almost boring, and I smiled at the irony: I had been interrogated more thoroughly by probation officers over faulty GPS alerts than I was by federal security before an international flight.

And then came the moment of truth—boarding El Al. I felt a surge of pride just seeing the blue-and-white tailfin. This wasn't just any airline; this was Israel's airline, a steel and jet-fueled extension of the flag I had carried through so many hostile streets.

The flight itself turned into an unexpected gift. El Al upgraded me to business class. A lay-flat seat. A massive screen. Warm meals served with care. And most importantly, a cabin manager named Ran who treated me like family the moment he saw me. He asked questions, offered reassurances, made sure I had everything I needed. For the first time in what felt like forever, I stretched out, closed my eyes, and allowed myself to feel something close to peace.

As the engines roared and Boston slipped away beneath the clouds, anticipation swelled in my chest. I wasn't just traveling. I was returning to the very land at the center of all of this. The place that had lit the fire inside me. Israel was no longer just a flag I waved in defiance. Now, it was just hours away.

Ben-Gurion Airport did not disappoint. Anyone who has flown into Israel knows the security interview process is less "customs" and more "cross-examination." There's no quick smile and stamp like in Europe. It's closer to an oral exam, where you don't know the subject matter until the questions start flying.

My greeting was more intense than most. Maybe it was my American passport. Maybe it was my last name. Maybe it was the way I looked—just a middle-aged guy flying solo, eyes wide with that unmistakable mix of nerves and excitement that only comes from stepping onto new ground you've dreamed about for years. For me, it wasn't just any destination. It was Israel. And not in a time of calm, when tour buses lined the streets of Jerusalem and cafés buzzed with chatter, but in the middle of a war.

Most people I knew thought I was crazy to go then. But I wasn't deterred. If anything, the pull was stronger. I'd seen Israel through headlines, through rallies, through prayers, but never with my own eyes. Now here I was, boarding a flight like a pilgrim who had shown up late but still believed he belonged.

Maybe it was that mix—vacationer's excitement colliding with wartime determination—that made me stand out. I wasn't blending in. I wasn't trying to. And apparently, that was enough to get me flagged.

The young security officer looked like she could've been my daughter's classmate—barely 22, hair pulled back tight, uniform sharp. But her eyes were sharpest of all.

"Why are you here?" she asked, her tone clipped, professional.

"Vacation," I said, flashing what I hoped was an easy smile. "With a friend."

"Name?"

I gave it.

"Where are they from?"

I answered.

"Where did you meet them?"

"Boston."

Her eyes narrowed. "How do you know them?"

"Rallies," I said, maybe too proudly.

Her pen stopped mid-stroke. She looked up, eyebrows raised. "Rallies?"

My stomach sank. My inner voice groaned: Nice work, Scott. You just told Israeli airport security you spend your free time hanging around at political rallies. That's not exactly the safe tourist answer they were fishing for.

So I leaned in, doubling down. "Pro-Israel rallies," I clarified quickly. "Against Hamas. Against antisemitism."

"What's your father's name? Your mother's? Your daughter? Where does she live? What do they do? What did you eat on the plane? Did you pack your own bag? Has anyone given you a gift?"

By minute 15, I felt like I was back in Army debriefs. By minute 20, I half expected her to ask me about my third-grade report card. Still, I understood. Every question, every skeptical glance, every follow-up wasn't personal—it was about keeping the country safe. Israel doesn't have the luxury of casual borders.

Finally, after what felt like an hour of pointed questions and long pauses while her pen scratched across the form, she looked up, nodded, and waved me through. I exhaled like I had just finished a marathon.

The glass doors slid open, and I stepped into the arrival hall. The air smelled different—dusty and dry, but alive. Even the hum of travelers, the swirl of Hebrew and English and Russian voices around me, felt electric. I grabbed a taxi with my friend, and we headed into Tel Aviv.

She had chosen perfectly: a fourth-floor apartment one block from the beach, with a balcony, a small kitchen, and three bedrooms. It wasn't fancy, but it was ours. From the balcony, you could see the rooftops sloping toward the sea, and at night, the city hummed with life just beneath our feet.

Our first day was overcast but warm—perfect walking weather. We wandered the length of the beach, toes skimming the Mediterranean, the water stretching endlessly toward Europe. Coffee stands popped up like oases, and kite surfers carved arcs into the waves. Tel Aviv didn't just move—it pulsed. By mid-morning, we had walked all the way up to the former U.S. Embassy, quieter now since the move to Jerusalem, but still carrying the weight of history.

That afternoon, we took a taxi to Hostage Square. If the beach had been freedom, Hostage Square was grief. Candles flickered, posters bore the faces of the kidnapped, and families sat in clusters, their pain visible but their dignity unshaken. I had seen their counterparts in Boston, at the terror tunnel exhibit the summer before, when I was entrusted to protect and host families of hostages. Standing there in Tel Aviv, surrounded by the very people I had fought for back home, it felt like the story had come full circle.

We ended our first day at a small bar just down the block from our Airbnb. The food was excellent, the drinks even better, but it was the staff who made it unforgettable. Over the next two weeks, that bar became our second home. The bartenders learned our names. The waiters sat with us during slow hours. Strangers became friends, and friends became family.

After the interrogations, the fights, the rallies, and the courtroom chaos, Tel Aviv gave me something I hadn't felt in a long time: belonging.

On our second morning in Israel, EK and I decided to set out on foot from our Airbnb. The Mediterranean stretched out before us as we walked along the seaside promenade, the water a deep, impossible blue, broken only by the white spray of waves hitting the rocks. Fishermen leaned over the railings with their lines in the water, while joggers and families strolled past, the city humming with its usual morning rhythm. There was a kind of electricity in the air—the awareness that life carried on, even with the war still looming overhead.

From the promenade we turned into Jaffa, letting the narrow alleys pull us in like a labyrinth. The stone walls rose up on either side, their centuries of history almost tangible. Every few steps another doorway tempted me—a shop crowded with colorful ceramics, another stacked with leather sandals, another draped with bright fabrics that swayed like banners in the dim light. The air was thick with cardamom and coffee, laced with the salt drifting in from the sea.

Somewhere in that maze I found a tiny wine shop. It wasn't much more than a single room stacked floor to ceiling with bottles, the owner, a lovely Russian woman, sat behind the counter. Without thinking much about it, I bought two liters, congratulating myself on such a "local" purchase. The victory faded quickly. As soon as I stepped back into the sun I realized I would be lugging those bottles around for the rest of the day. With every turn of the alley they seemed to grow heavier, the straps pulling at my shoulders in time with my footsteps—a constant reminder of my own impulsive shopping.

Later that afternoon I made my way toward Tel Aviv's Shuk HaCarmel. If Jaffa's alleys had felt like a maze, the shuk was a storm—louder, faster, alive in a way that nearly bowled me over. The moment I stepped inside, I was swallowed by the noise. Vendors shouted over one another in rapid-fire Hebrew, their voices tumbling and colliding until it felt like the whole street was vibrating. Bargaining mixed with laughter, with the crash of crates being stacked, with the buzz of a thousand conversations fighting to be heard.

The smells hit just as hard. Spices—cumin, coriander, cinnamon—hung heavy in the air, mingling with roasted nuts, fried dough, and meat sizzling over open flames. One stall reeked of dried fish, the next bloomed with the sweetness of pomegranates bursting open, their juice staining the counters. Somewhere in the chaos, the sharp, earthy bite of fresh coffee cut through it all.

But it wasn't just the market itself that made the place feel electric—it was the urgency in the air. It was Friday afternoon, and Shabbat was coming. People weren't just shopping, they were racing against the sun. Hands grabbed at stacks of challah braided in golden coils, customers barked out last-minute orders for roasted chickens, and families moved like units, kids tugging at sleeves while parents hurriedly filled bags. There was no time to linger; every purchase was a small battle against the clock.

The crowd pressed in on all sides, a restless tide carrying me along whether I wanted to move or not. I tried to keep pace, clutching my bag, my eyes darting from trays of sticky pastries glistening with syrup to baskets overflowing with olives in every shade of green and black. My senses couldn't keep up.

For a moment, I stopped in the middle of it all, letting the wave flow around me. The shuk wasn't just a marketplace—it was the pulse of Tel Aviv on the edge of Shabbat. It was noisy, sweaty, and overwhelming, but it was also beautiful. This was the rhythm of people preparing to stop, to rest, to breathe. And here I was, right in the middle of it, experiencing that heartbeat for the very first time.

The next adventure came when EK decided to go kite boarding, leaving me with a free afternoon in Tel Aviv. I had already been thinking about a tattoo for some time, something permanent to mark this trip and my commitment to stand with the Jewish people. It wasn't a spur-of-the-moment decision. I had debated it for weeks, and once I knew I was coming to Israel, I researched studios online. Dynamo Tattoo kept coming up—clean work, good reviews, and a reputation that made me feel confident.

So when I found myself with those free hours, I walked through their door with intention. The studio had the crisp, sterile smell of ink and disinfectant, balanced by a low hum of music. The artists worked with quiet focus, their walls lined with sketches and photographs of past pieces. I told them what I wanted: a Star of David, black ink, centered on my chest just below my neckline. Bold, visible, not something to be hidden.

The artist nodded, sketched the design with practiced ease, and soon I was stretched out under the buzzing needle. The pain was sharp but steady, manageable, almost grounding. I watched as the lines took shape, simple and strong. When it was finished, I looked in the mirror and saw it there—clean, stark, unmistakable. A black Star of David, right over the center of my chest.

It wasn't just a tattoo. It was a declaration, a reminder etched into my skin of the choice I had made long before setting foot in Israel: to stand openly, permanently, with the Jewish people.

The next morning we set out for a full day trip with Amit Musaei, a survivor of the October 7th Nova festival massacre. Riding beside him, listening to his quiet explanations, I felt the gravity of being guided by someone who had lived through the unthinkable. Our first stop was Sderot, a city pressed right up against the Gaza border, its skyline and soundscape forever shaped by proximity to war.

From the overlook you could both see and hear the conflict unfolding in real time. The thud of distant artillery carried on the wind, followed by the echo of explosions rolling across the flat fields. Even though we were outside the immediate danger zone, the sound had weight; it pressed into your chest. Amit didn't flinch. For him, it was familiar. For me, it was jarring—a reminder that in Sderot, war isn't a headline, it's the background noise of daily life.

The city itself bore the marks of October 7. Amit pointed out the site where the police station once stood, demolished during the battle that day when Hamas fighters stormed Sderot. What had been a place of authority and protection was reduced to rubble and ash. The loss wasn't just physical—it was symbolic. On that morning, the heart of the city had been ripped out, and everyone here knew it.

Walking the streets, I noticed something that at first seemed out of place, until I realized it was everywhere: bomb shelters. Every few hundred feet, sometimes painted brightly with murals to soften their presence, sometimes raw and gray, they stood ready. In playgrounds, outside schools, beside markets—they were as common as bus stops. For residents of Sderot, they weren't emergency infrastructure. They were as essential to life as sidewalks.

Standing there, the explosions rumbling in the distance, I tried to imagine living with that kind of reality day after day. For Amit and the people of Sderot, it wasn't imagination. It was life—resilient, scarred, and unrelenting.

From Sderot we drove south, the fields flattening into wide stretches of land until Amit turned us off onto a dirt road. There was no sign, no marker to tell you where you were headed, but he knew the way by memory, a memory seared into him. Soon we arrived at the Nova festival site.

Even before we got out, I felt the heaviness in the air. This wasn't just a field—it was sacred ground, haunted ground. Amit led us slowly, his voice steady but carrying the kind of weight only a survivor can. He told us where the stages had been, where the dancing stopped and the terror began. He didn't embellish. He didn't need to. His story was carved into the earth.

Some of the festival infrastructure was still standing, ghostlike reminders of joy turned to horror. A bar stood in place, silent now, its counters once alive with music and laughter but also the site where young people had been gunned down. Nearby, the hulking shape of a big yellow dumpster sat in the dirt. Amit told us how some had tried to hide inside, desperate for safety, only to be found and murdered. The sight of it was almost unbearable in its ordinariness—something so mundane turned into a coffin.

Everywhere, the land was marked with memorials. Photographs and flowers lined makeshift shrines, each face smiling, frozen in time. Friends had left bracelets, notes, candles—tokens of love and grief clinging to this open space. The wind lifted dust across the ground, and as it swirled, it felt as though it carried with it the names and stories of those who had been killed here.

Standing beside Amit as he spoke, I realized how impossible it was to separate the place from the people. This wasn't just a field or an event site.

It was a mass graveyard, a scar in the earth and in the heart of Israel. And yet, in Amit's voice, there was something more than sorrow—there was defiance, a refusal to let the memory of that day be reduced to statistics or headlines. Here, every grain of dust seemed to whisper the truth: they were young, they were alive, and they were stolen by Hamas.

I listened, I looked, and I carried the weight of it in silence.

From Nova, we drove to the burnt vehicles compound. At first it looked like an ordinary lot—rows of metal and wire, the kind of place you'd expect to see old buses or scrap. But as soon as we walked in, the scale of it hit me. This wasn't scrap. These were the remains of lives violently cut short.

Row after row of twisted steel stood like a graveyard. Cars collapsed into themselves, blackened shells that had once been filled with music, laughter, the ordinary clutter of road trips and weekends away. The smell of burned metal still lingered faintly, even over a year later, carried in the air like smoke that refused to fade.

Some vehicles were riddled with bullet holes, their windows shattered, doors scarred from the force of impact. Others were melted into shapes that barely resembled cars anymore—roofs caved in, frames buckled, rubber wheels gone to ash. Here and there sat ambulances, stripped of color, the red cross still visible through the soot. They hadn't been spared.

I walked slowly, taking it all in, trying not to imagine but failing anyway. A car seat still clung to the back of one vehicle, warped by heat. An air freshener dangled from a mirror, half-burned but somehow still there. Little traces of lives interrupted, frozen in ruin.

It was overwhelming. Each vehicle seemed to hum with a story I couldn't hear but could feel pressing down on me. These weren't just cars—they were evidence. They were witnesses. They were proof of what had been done, and they stood in rows as if demanding the world not look away.

I didn't. I couldn't. The compound was a testament, and standing in the middle of it I understood again why I was here. To see, to carry, to tell.

Our last stop that day was Shuva Junction, a kind of way station for soldiers rotating in and out of Gaza. From the road it looked unassuming, just a cluster of tents and makeshift stations, but as soon as we stepped in, I realized it was something extraordinary. Volunteers moved quickly from table to table, their faces lit with purpose. There were hot meals steaming on long folding tables, stacks of bottled water and energy drinks, crates of socks and toiletries, even massage chairs lined up under a tarp where exhausted young soldiers leaned back, eyes closed, trying to steal a moment of rest.

It wasn't military infrastructure. It was community, pure and unfiltered. Ordinary Israelis—mothers, fathers, retirees, teenagers—had built this oasis for the soldiers, a place where they could shed the dust and the weight of combat for just a little while.

Amit led me through the bustle and introduced me to a young IDF soldier, fresh from the front. His uniform was dusty, his face drawn with fatigue, but when Amit explained that I was a U.S. veteran, something changed. He stood a little taller, eyes brightening, and without hesitation he took off his hat. It was worn, sweat-stained, with his unit patch stitched across the front—something personal, something earned. He pressed it into my hands.

"This is for you," he said simply.

I was caught off guard. It was a gesture of trust, of kinship that went deeper than words. I reached up, took the Red Sox hat I'd been wearing all day—faded, broken in, a piece of home—and handed it to him. He grinned as he put it on, adjusting the brim like it had always been his.

For a moment, standing there at Shuva Junction, the chaos of war faded. It was just two soldiers, two veterans, exchanging hats as a sign of respect. Different countries, different uniforms, but bound by something universal: service, sacrifice, and the unspoken understanding that comes with both.

As we left, I looked down at the hat in my hands, the unit patch rough beneath my fingers. It wasn't just a souvenir. It was a symbol of connection, of solidarity—something I would carry home, just as I carried the weight of everything I had seen that day.

The next day, I was invited by the head of Betar USA to visit the Jabotinsky Institute in Tel Aviv. For me, this wasn't just a museum visit—it was a pilgrimage. The moment I walked through the doors, I felt the shift. This wasn't simply an archive of dusty artifacts; it was a living reminder of one man's vision, and of the movement that shaped generations.

Betar was never just a youth movement. It was a crucible—a place where Jewish boys and girls were taught courage, discipline, and an uncompromising pride in who they were. At a time when Jews around the world were being told to shrink themselves, to disappear, Jabotinsky's movement raised them to stand tall, to fight if they had to, and to never apologize for existing.

As I moved through the exhibits, I felt as though I was walking through layers of purpose. Photographs of young men in crisp uniforms, flags bearing the proud insignia, letters written in Jabotinsky's own hand—all of it radiated a kind of steel that was both inspiring and sobering. These weren't abstract ideas on the wall; they were instructions for survival, blueprints for resilience.

One room held items from the Jewish Legion, the force Jabotinsky had helped raise during the First World War. Seeing their uniforms and weapons displayed, I couldn't help but feel the echo of my own military past. The parallel was impossible to ignore: men and women who had volunteered, not because it was easy or safe, but because they believed their people's future demanded it.

What struck me most was how Jabotinsky's voice still seemed to reach across the decades. His words, etched on placards and woven through the exhibits, carried an urgency that hadn't faded. He understood that Jewish survival required more than prayer or hope—it required action, backbone, and the courage to meet hatred head-on.

Standing there, I realized this was more than history. It was instruction. It was a reminder that resolve is not inherited; it is chosen, reaffirmed every generation, and every day. And for me, at that moment, it was reaffirmed again.

Israeli Independence Day was unlike anything I had ever experienced. In the United States, national holidays often blur together—cookouts, fireworks, maybe a parade—but here, remembrance carried a weight you could feel in the air. The day didn't start with celebration. It began with silence.

When the sirens sounded, the entire country froze. It wasn't a gradual pause; it was immediate, absolute. Cars on the highway pulled to the shoulder, drivers stepping out and standing at attention beside their vehicles. Pedestrians stopped mid-stride, conversations cut off mid-sentence. Even children fell quiet. For two minutes, life in Israel simply stopped.

I stood among them, listening to the long, mournful wail of the sirens stretch across the city. The sound wasn't just noise—it was memory. It was grief, respect, and defiance woven together. In those moments, time itself seemed suspended, as if the entire nation had agreed to step outside of daily life and stand united in remembrance.

Looking around, what struck me most was not the silence itself but the stillness of it. No one fidgeted. No one checked their phone. No one tried to slip past unnoticed. Whether on a crowded street in Tel Aviv or an empty stretch of highway in the Galilee, everyone participated. It wasn't enforced—it was embodied.

And then, as suddenly as it had begun, the sirens faded. The country exhaled. Cars started again, conversations resumed, footsteps picked up. Life continued, but with the weight of those two minutes carried forward.

For me, it was one of the most powerful moments of the trip. In America, remembrance is often personal, private, fragmented. Here, it was collective. The entire nation turned itself into a living memorial, if only for two minutes. And in those minutes, I understood something I had always believed but never fully seen: Israel remembers together, and it survives together.

Later that Independence Day, I was invited to a friend's family home in Herzliya for a barbecue. Asaf was someone I'd met through a Breitling watch group, one of those unexpected connections that seem small at first but end up shaping your journey. Now here I was, not just shaking his hand but sitting in his yard, surrounded by his kids and relatives, folded into the rhythm of their holiday.

The grill was already going when I arrived, smoke curling into the afternoon air. Platters of meat and vegetables lined the table—skewers of chicken and beef, bright peppers and onions, thick cuts of steak sizzling over the coals. The smell alone was intoxicating, the kind of rich, savory smoke that clings to your clothes and tells you you're in the right place.

Asaf's family moved around me with the effortless hospitality Israelis seem to carry in their bones. Plates were pressed into my hands before I could ask, glasses refilled the moment they were half-empty. His kids darted in and out, laughing, tugging at his sleeve, occasionally daring to practice a word or two of English with me before running off again.

We ate until we couldn't anymore, the food coming in waves—fresh salads bright with herbs, warm pita, grilled vegetables bursting with flavor, and of course, more meat pulled from the fire and sliced thin onto waiting plates. Everything was shared, passed around the table, no one ever left out.

What struck me most was how natural it felt to be included. I wasn't a visitor anymore; I was a guest, which in Israel means something deeper. Israeli hospitality doesn't stop at offering you food and drink. It folds you into the family, even if only for a night. Sitting there, watching his kids spray foam at each other, I realized this was the true heart of Independence Day: not just the stillness of remembrance or the spectacle of celebration, but the warmth of gathering around a table, side by side, alive, together.

Next on our trip we went to Akko, an ancient port city where history doesn't just sit in museums—it's pressed into the very stones underfoot. Every wall, every arch, seemed to carry the weight of centuries. It was a place where cultures and empires had risen and fallen, leaving their fingerprints behind. Phoenicians, Romans, Crusaders, Ottomans—all had passed through, and somehow the city still lived and breathed in its own rhythm.

What struck me most was how Akko was still, in every sense, a mixed city. Arabs and Jews, Muslims and Christians, markets and mosques and churches all coexisted within its walls. Sometimes it felt like harmony, with neighbors chatting over baskets of fruit or children darting between stalls, and sometimes you could sense the tension just beneath the surface. But it was real life, not staged, and that gave the city a raw honesty I couldn't shake.

The market streets were alive with sound and smell. Narrow alleys overflowed with spices—pyramids of turmeric and saffron glowing gold and red under the sun, piles of za'atar and dried chilies perfuming the air. Fishmongers laid out their catch on cracked slabs of ice, their voices competing with the calls of vendors selling sweets drenched in syrup. The air was salty, pungent, and alive.

I walked through the Crusader tunnels, stooping beneath heavy stone ceilings that once sheltered knights preparing for battle. The air was cool and damp, carrying the echo of footsteps across centuries. Emerging back into the light, I climbed the ramparts and stood overlooking the sea, the waves crashing against walls that had seen sieges, prayers, and pilgrimages. It was humbling to realize that the same stones had witnessed not only war and conquest, but also quiet moments of devotion and community life that never made the history books.

Akko wasn't polished, and that was its power. It was messy, layered, human—a city where past and present pressed against each other without apology. Walking its streets, I felt both like an outsider and a participant, swept into the endless story the city was still telling.

Her family picked us up in Akko, and with that, the day shifted. We had spent hours inside the old city's weight—alleys pressed with spice and salt, stone walls breathing history—and now we were folded into the rhythm of family, climbing into the car and heading out of town.

Not long after, we stopped at a highway rest stop that looked, from the outside, like nothing special—just a gas station with a small café attached. But inside, we were served hummus that changed everything I thought I knew about the dish. It was impossibly smooth, almost creamy, with tahini, garlic, and lemon singing in balance. Warm pita came straight from the oven, puffed and blistered just enough, and together it was perfection. I couldn't help but laugh: after wandering through ancient port cities and centuries-old markets, the best hummus I'd ever had came from a roadside gas station.

The coast fell behind as we drove east, and the scenery shifted with every mile. The wide horizon of the sea gave way to rolling hills, terraces carved into the earth, and villages perched on ridges. The air cooled as we climbed, the colors of the land deepening with the late afternoon light. By the time we reached their home, the valley stretched out beneath us, dotted with olive groves and the clustered rooftops of nearby towns.

That evening, I sat behind the house, looking out over the hills as the day folded into dusk. The air was still, carrying the faint trace of smoke from nearby kitchens. Then, rising from the town of Sha'ab in the valley below, the call to prayer began. The sound drifted upward, lingering and echoing across the hills. It wasn't jarring—it was melodic, almost haunting, a reminder that life here was layered, ancient, and ongoing.

When night finally came, I slept in the *mamad*—the reinforced safe room built into every Israeli home. It was quiet, thicker-walled than anywhere else in the house, a cocoon of silence. After days of movement, noise, and crowded streets, I sank into sleep almost instantly. Morning came late for me; the sun was already streaming in when I opened my eyes. I had overslept, and realized with a kind of gratitude that it was because, for the first time in a long while, I had slept in absolute peace.

The next day with her family took us north, climbing toward the Lebanese border. The scenery changed as the road rose and fell, the coastline stretching below us in jagged cliffs and waves smashing themselves white against the rocks. From that height the Mediterranean looked endless, a vast expanse of blue meeting the horizon, and it was beautiful—until the quiet broke.

As we drove, the air raid sirens blared across the town, the family exchanging glances that carried no panic, only routine. For me, it was new and jarring. Her uncle eased the car to the side of the road. We got out quickly, moving into position as if it were second nature for them, but for me it felt surreal. We crouched low by a wall on a not so busy street, waiting for the all-clear. My heart pounded, adrenaline spiking, but around me no one seemed afraid. This was life here, something Israelis had been practicing for decades, woven into the rhythm of daily existence. To me, it was anything but ordinary.

When the danger passed, we climbed back into the car and continued, the conversation resuming as if nothing had happened. I sat quietly, absorbing the strangeness of it—how normal it could be to live on the edge of something so threatening.

Later, winding back through the Galilee, we stopped at a Druze village where the air smelled of smoke and spice. At the roadside, a woman worked over a heated dome, flattening dough into wide, thin circles of bread. She spread labneh across it, sprinkled za'atar and other herbs in generous handfuls, then rolled it up into something that looked simple but tasted unforgettable. The bread was warm and soft, the labneh tangy and cool, the spice blend earthy and sharp all at once. I stood there eating with my hands, watching cars pass on the narrow road, realizing this was as much Israel as the rocket warnings had been—fear and threat on one side, hospitality and flavor on the other.

That day left me unsettled but also strangely grounded. The land wasn't just layered with history—it was layered with contrast, with lives lived between danger and resilience, between war and bread, between the edge of survival and the comfort of something homemade and shared.

During the trip, I had the honor of meeting Hillel Fuld, one of Israel's most prominent tech entrepreneurs and influencers. Sitting across from him over coffee, I was struck by the way his energy fused faith, innovation, and Zionism into one seamless conviction. He didn't separate them—he lived them as one. He spoke about startups and Torah in the same breath, about Israel not only as a safe haven but as the engine of ideas that could change the world. Listening to him, I realized that Zionism is not only defensive; it is forward-looking. It isn't just about survival—it's about thriving, building, and leading. His vision reminded me that to stand for Israel is to stand for possibility itself.

The day I set out for Jerusalem began like any other train ride, until it didn't. At Savidor station in Tel Aviv, the loudspeaker cut through the crowd with a sharp announcement, and almost instantly the sirens began. An incoming rocket alert. The easy shuffle of commuters shifted to urgency. People moved quickly but without panic, funneling into the reinforced shelters at the station. I followed, heart thudding, trying to keep pace with those who had done this countless times before.

We waited. The air was tense, hushed except for the faint sound of someone's phone buzzing with updates. A few minutes later the all-clear sounded. Life resumed as if a switch had been flipped. People filed back up to the platforms, and I boarded the next train toward Jerusalem.

We didn't get far. Two stops in, the train halted. An announcement followed: service was suspended. No more trains would continue to Jerusalem. At first it was just an inconvenience—an interruption, a change of plans—but as the minutes dragged into hours, the reason became clearer. A missile had landed near Ben-Gurion Airport, and the authorities didn't want more people crowding transport hubs or moving closer to potential targets.

So there we were, stranded at a small station, two hours or so of waiting with no real answers. IDF soldiers filled the platforms and benches, their rifles slung casually across their shoulders, their presence both reassuring and surreal. They were stranded too, just like the rest of us—young men and women in uniform, stuck waiting for the next move.

The scene carried a strange mix of calm and tension. Some soldiers joked with each other, sharing snacks and scrolling through their phones. Others leaned against the walls, eyes distant, maybe already back in Gaza in their minds. For me, the waiting was heavy. I kept replaying the chain of events in my head—the sirens, the shelter, the sudden halt—as if trying to make sense of being caught in a rhythm that, for Israelis, was all too familiar.

When the next train finally came through, relief rippled across the platform. We boarded quietly, as though all of us understood that this ride wasn't routine anymore—it was survival, patience, resilience all stitched into the simple act of continuing forward.

Jerusalem is a city that resists definition. It is ancient and modern, sacred and chaotic, eternal and fragile, all at once. Its stones are worn smooth by the countless feet of pilgrims who have crossed its narrow streets for millennia. Walking there feels less like moving forward in time and more like moving through it—layer by layer, prayer by prayer.

We wandered through its many dimensions: the Via Dolorosa, where Christians retrace the final steps of Jesus; the Church of the Holy Sepulchre, heavy with incense and devotion; the Jewish Quarter, alive with laughter, mezuzahs on every doorway; the Temple Mount, tense with history and contested faith. Every corner whispered a different story. Every wall carried a claim.

But nothing compared to standing before the Western Wall. As I approached, I placed a simple Chabad kippah on my head, folded a small handwritten prayer into my palm, and pressed my forehead against the cool, ancient stone. The weight of the place was overwhelming—here, on the foundation of the First and Second Temples, generations had poured their hearts out to God. I added mine: for justice in my own life, for Israel's safety, for peace for the Jewish people. Slipping the paper into a crack between the stones felt like joining a chorus thousands of years old, voices that had never gone silent no matter how much the world tried to erase them.

And yet, even in this place of timeless holiness, Israel's fragility made itself known. Halfway through my trip, sirens pierced the air—a rocket had been launched by the Houthis in Yemen. For a moment, the abstract became real. The crowd around me moved with calm precision, like they had rehearsed this their whole lives. People found shelter, checked on one another, and waited.

Minutes later, life resumed as if nothing had happened. Cafés reopened. Children laughed in the streets. That night, the bar down the block from our Airbnb was packed, music spilling into the night air. It wasn't indifference—it was resilience. A refusal to let fear dictate life.

That contrast stayed with me: pressing my prayer into ancient stone one day, hearing sirens the next. In Israel, eternity and immediacy coexist. The wall endures, the rockets fall, and the people keep living. Hope is not abstract here—it's daily, stubborn, defiant.

Visiting Yad Vashem was unlike anything else I experienced in Israel. The approach itself set the tone: the museum rose out of the hillside, sharp lines of concrete cutting into the earth, as if the building itself carried the weight of memory. From the moment I stepped inside, I felt the air shift—quieter, heavier, reverent.

The exhibits unfolded like a journey through darkness. Photographs, letters, and artifacts told the story of European Jewry before the Holocaust, vibrant communities alive with culture and tradition, before they were stripped away piece by piece. The rooms grew narrower, more suffocating, as the story deepened into ghettos, deportations, and the machinery of extermination. Glass cases displayed shoes, prayer books, children's toys—ordinary objects made unbearable by the knowledge of what had followed.

What struck me most wasn't just the scale of loss, but the resilience threaded through it. Testimonies of resistance and survival were carved into the narrative—uprisings, clandestine schools, Jews who risked their lives to preserve a shred of dignity in the face of annihilation. It wasn't only a story of victimhood. It was also a story of strength.

Outside, in the Garden of the Righteous Among the Nations, plaques honored non-Jews who had risked everything to save Jewish lives. Trees grew tall and steady along the path, each one a living memorial to courage. Names from across Europe—Polish farmers, Dutch families, French priests—stood in quiet defiance of the idea that the world had stood by in silence. They reminded me that even in humanity's darkest hour, there were lights that refused to go out.

I lingered at the Hall of Names, which contained a massive book with every name—millions of names of the murdered, with empty shelves for those still unrecorded. Standing there, surrounded by their memory, I felt the enormity of the Holocaust in a way no book or film had ever conveyed.

And in that silence, my resolve deepened. This wasn't history to me anymore—it was a charge. I thought of the star inked into my chest, of my decision to stand openly with the Jewish people, and in that moment it felt less like a personal choice and more like a responsibility. If the world could allow this to happen once, then anyone who claims to stand with Israel, with the Jewish people, has to mean it with their whole being.

Walking back into the sunlight, I carried with me both the weight of horror and the strength of survival. Yad Vashem wasn't only about remembering what had been lost—it was about ensuring that memory becomes action. For me, it wasn't optional anymore. I would stand with the Jewish people not just in words, but in life. Their story was now part of mine.

Two weeks slipped through my fingers like sand on the Tel Aviv shore. When the time came to leave, I carried far more than a suitcase. My phone overflowed with pictures—too many of cats lounging on cars and rooftops, of sunsets over the Mediterranean, of meals that felt less like eating and more like communion. But what I truly carried was intangible:

conversations that cut straight to the soul, laughter that felt like healing, and a love for Israel that had deepened into something immovable.

Saying goodbye hurt in a way I hadn't anticipated. I had come as a visitor, but I left feeling grafted into something ancient and alive, something that claimed me as much as I claimed it. Israel wasn't just a place I had traveled to—it was a place that had entered me, reshaped me.

Israel reminded me why I fight. Not only in rallies, not only in courtrooms, but in my heart. Because this land and these people embody the truth I have staked my life on: the Jewish people are eternal, and so is their homeland.

Leaving Israel wasn't simply the end of a trip. It was a crossing of thresholds. For two weeks, I had lived in a place where Jewish life wasn't tolerated—it was the default, the foundation, the unapologetic norm. No one questioned why I carried a flag or why I raised my voice. No one tried to criminalize survival. In Israel, the question wasn't *if* Jews should exist; it was how best to keep thriving.

Back in Massachusetts, everything was inverted. There, I had defended Jewish life and been turned into a defendant. There, the DA twisted survival into criminality. In Israel, people thanked me for standing tall. At home, prosecutors and politicians tried to break me for the same act.

The contrast was staggering. In Jerusalem, I stood before stones that had outlasted empires, feeling the prayers of generations pulsing beneath my hands. In Tel Aviv, I felt joy as resilience—people dancing, building, living. On the border, I felt tension but also unflinching resolve. And in Hostage Square, surrounded by families of the kidnapped, I saw pain carried with dignity, grief transformed into defiance.

It was there that clarity crystallized. My battle in Newton was not separate from Israel's battle. It was the same war, fought on different terrain—a war over survival, over dignity, over the right to exist unapologetically. If hostage families could endure unimaginable loss and still demand justice, how could I not endure false charges? If Israel could rise from ashes into a nation, how could I not rise from the smear campaign of a DA's office?

As the plane lifted from Ben-Gurion, I pressed my forehead to the window and watched the coastline fade. I knew what awaited me: job applications that would go unanswered, prosecutors who still circled, headlines that still branded me. But I also knew I wasn't returning empty-handed.

I carried prayers tucked into the Wall. I carried the flicker of candles at Hostage Square. I carried the laughter of friends in a Tel Aviv bar, the sound of waves against the shore, the resilience of a people who have endured worse than false accusations.

Israel gave me more than memories. It gave me perspective. It gave me hope. It gave me the strength to see my own trial not as a desperate attempt to clear my name, but as my place in a larger story—an unbroken chain of a people who will not bow, who will not break, who will not vanish.

When I stepped back onto American soil, I wasn't the same man who had left. I had gone to Israel searching for escape. I came back with a mission. A mission to fight with the same defiance I had seen etched in Jerusalem's stones and lived out on Tel Aviv's streets.

Because Israel taught me that survival is not enough. We must live. We must fight. And above all, we must do so with pride.

But as the wheels of my plane touched down in Boston, I felt it—the weight of unfinished business pressing back onto my shoulders. The trial loomed. The headlines still circled. Marian Ryan and her office hadn't gone away.

Israel had given me strength. Now Massachusetts would test it.

The fight wasn't over. It was only just beginning.

Chapter 18:
Witch Hunt — Marian Ryan's Revenge

When people ask me what the most shocking part of my ordeal was, they usually expect me to talk about the attack itself—the split-second when a man launched himself at me, when I twisted to shield my pistol, when survival hinged on a trigger pull. But the truth is this: the most disturbing moment wasn't on that sidewalk. It came afterward, in the cold fluorescence of the legal system, when Middlesex County District Attorney Marian Ryan decided to turn me from victim into villain.

Make no mistake: Marian Ryan's betrayal of justice cut deeper than the bruises on my body. I had prepared my entire adult life for the possibility of combat, for the possibility of violence, for the split-second decisions that can mean life or death. What I hadn't prepared for—what no training could prepare me for—was to be treated like a criminal after surviving an attempted killing.

Ryan was no stranger to twisting the law to fit her agenda. In Massachusetts legal circles, she had already earned a reputation as a staunch anti-gun crusader, a prosecutor who saw every firearm not as a tool but as a threat—and every gun owner not as a citizen but as a suspect. She wore the mantle of the "progressive prosecutor," a phrase that sounds noble until you see what it really means: weaponizing the courts to pursue ideology, not justice. She was proudly in the mold of George Soros–backed prosecutors who have spread across America's cities—more interested in press releases than public safety, more concerned with headlines than fairness, more invested in optics than in truth.

And in my case, she followed that script to the letter.

I wasn't just charged. I was made into a political pawn, a convenient headline for a DA desperate to burnish her progressive credentials. Instead of acknowledging that I had defended myself, my friends, and the public from a violent attacker, Ryan saw an opportunity to send a message: in Middlesex County, lawful self-defense with a firearm would be treated as a crime.

That was the real shock. Not the fight for my life on the pavement. Not the concussion, the bruises, the broken watch, the shattered sunglasses. The real shock was watching the very system I once trusted contort itself into a weapon—not against the man who attacked me, but against me, for daring to survive.

Within hours of the Newton incident—an attack where I lawfully defended myself against a violent, ideologically driven aggressor—I was no longer being treated as the victim. I was painted as the criminal. The charges that came down weren't just heavy-handed—they were absurd. Assault and battery with a dangerous weapon. And worse—a civil rights violation. A civil rights violation—for defending myself at a pro-Israel rally, while being assaulted by a man who crossed the street screaming antisemitic threats, lunging at me, and clawing for my firearm.

That charge wasn't just legally reckless; it was obscene. It turned reality on its head. The man trying to maim me became the supposed "victim," while I—the one who survived—was branded the oppressor. It was political theater masquerading as law.

And the speed of it all revealed the truth. Even before I was arraigned, Ryan's office was working overtime to spin a narrative: not about facts, not about evidence, but about optics. They needed a villain, and I was convenient. It was swift, calculated, and entirely in service of preserving Marian Ryan's political image and pandering to the increasingly radical left that controls Massachusetts politics.

What made it even more infuriating was that this wasn't some one-off mistake, some lapse in judgment. Ryan had a track record of weaponizing the law against people trying to defend themselves. Her incompetence and ideology were already on the record for the world to see.

Take *Commonwealth v. Caetano* (2016). Jaime Caetano, a woman abused and terrorized by her ex-boyfriend, carried a stun gun to protect herself. Ryan's office prosecuted her for it, pushing to uphold Massachusetts' total ban on stun guns. Think about that: instead of recognizing a battered woman's right to defend her life, Ryan made her the criminal. Her argument went all the way to the U.S. Supreme Court—and was shredded. In a rare, unanimous rebuke, the Court ruled that the Second Amendment protects *all* bearable arms, including modern tools like stun guns. Ryan's position wasn't just wrong—it was unconstitutional. She was embarrassed on the national stage, exposed as a prosecutor more interested in control than justice.

But here's the kicker: she learned nothing. Fast forward to Newton, and she used the same playbook. Target the victim. Twist the law. Criminalize self-defense. Package it neatly for the press. She had been humiliated once before by the Supreme Court, and still, she doubled down—this time at my expense.

And it's not just incompetence—it's endangerment. When prosecutors punish people for defending themselves, they send a clear message: *don't resist, don't fight back, submit.* That doesn't make communities safer. It makes them prey. It emboldens abusers, criminals, and ideologues, because they know the system won't stop them—and might even shield them. Marian Ryan's brand of "progressive prosecution" doesn't just fail victims. It actively *creates* more of them.

In Caetano's case, it meant a battered woman was dragged into court for daring to survive. In mine, it meant I was shackled, humiliated, and vilified for protecting my life and the lives of others. In both, the message was the same: politics above justice, ideology above truth, headlines above human safety.

That is Marian Ryan's legacy. And unless it's confronted, more lives will be shattered under the weight of her ambition.

Despite overwhelming evidence pointing to clear self-defense—video footage, eyewitness accounts, and the fact that I had no criminal history—Marian Ryan rushed to charge me harshly and publicly. The move wasn't just questionable; it was reckless. Legal observers across Massachusetts took notice. Alan Dershowitz, never one to mince words, openly asked why the case was even being brought in the first place. If one of Harvard's most prominent legal minds could see the absurdity at a glance, what possible excuse did Ryan have?

The answer, I would soon learn, wasn't law. It was politics.

From the very beginning, this case was never about what happened on that bridge in Newton. It was about headlines, optics, and Ryan's desire to posture as the "progressive prosecutor" willing to take on a man with a gun—even when that man had acted to save his own life.

Over the months that followed, my legal team waged what could only be described as a war of attrition with the Middlesex DA's office. Meeting after meeting, document after document, evidence stacked upon evidence—all of it pointed to the same conclusion: I had done nothing wrong.

They questioned the position of my hand on the firearm. We slowed the video down frame by frame and showed them the truth. They speculated about the timing of the draw. We laid out training standards, police procedure, combat instinct. They whispered about my intent. We brought rabbis, veterans, civic leaders, neighbors—people who could testify to my character, my restraint, my values.

None of it mattered. Ryan wasn't after the truth. She was after leverage.

Beginning in November 2024, her office floated so-called "off-ramps"—ways to resolve the case short of trial. But every proposal was poisoned. They weren't compromises; they were demands for submission.

Ryan wanted me barred from Newton indefinitely, as though I were the threat—not the man who ambushed me, but me. She wanted me to carry labels of wrongdoing I did not deserve, to accept punishments that would live forever in the record, not because they were justified, but because they were politically convenient for her.

Let me be crystal clear: Newton wasn't just another town on a map. Newton is home to thousands of Jewish families. It was the ground where I was attacked for standing with them. For Marian Ryan to insist I stay away from Newton was more than insulting—it was a warning shot to the Jewish community. The message was clear: if you defend yourself, if you dare to stand visibly as a Jew or with the Jewish people, *you may be the one punished*. That was the real danger in her terms.

And still, I tried to meet her halfway. I offered to stay out of Newton for one year—no more. I had already endured the ankle monitor digging into my leg, the sleepless nights from false GPS alerts, the humiliation of house arrest, the loss of work, the character assassination in the press. I had followed every rule they set before me. But still, it wasn't enough. They wanted more submission, more punishment, more bending of the knee.

In January 2025, my attorneys walked into what we thought would be the final meeting at the DA's office in Woburn. We laid it all out—again. The video evidence. The legal precedents. The character witnesses. The good-faith offers. At one point, even members of her own staff quietly conceded that I had likely acted in self-defense. But Marian Ryan still refused to sign off. She wanted more time. More restrictions. More headlines.

That was the moment I reached my breaking point. I told my attorneys: *This is it. This is the final offer. If they won't accept it, we go to trial. No more delays. No more manipulation. No more games.*

Because justice isn't found in half-measures or political bargaining. And I wasn't about to let a DA's ambition rewrite the truth of what happened that day.

We scheduled a court appearance to finalize what should have been a simple agreement. It had taken months of wrangling, back-and-forth proposals, and endless "revisions," but finally, we thought we were done. All that was left was to stand before the judge, confirm the terms, and close this exhausting chapter.

But the day before the hearing, Ryan's office pulled out—again. Their excuse? They suddenly objected to the wording of the Newton exclusion. We had deliberately left the final phrasing to the judge, the neutral arbiter, where it belonged. But that was exactly what Ryan feared. If the judge ruled against her, she would lose face. She couldn't risk another public embarrassment, so she torpedoed the deal at the eleventh hour.

That was my breaking point. No more games. No more delays. No more manipulation. *I demanded a trial.*

The judge, visibly fed up with the endless stalling, finally cut through the nonsense. A date was set: June 18, 2025. After months of shadowboxing, it was time for the real fight. We chose a bench trial unbeknownst to the DA, but publicly called for a jury trial, to have them waste time and effort in that direction then pull the carpet out from under their feet at the last moment. In Massachusetts, where lawful firearm ownership is demonized and pro-Israel sentiment is routinely politicized, putting my fate in the hands of twelve jurors carried too much risk. A judge, we believed, could at least evaluate the facts and the law without being swayed by emotion, propaganda, or prejudice.

Ryan's office scrambled. Stripped of a coherent case, they resorted to desperation. In a last-ditch effort, they tried to dredge up old social media posts—irrelevant tweets and comments from months before the incident. It had nothing to do with what happened on September 12. It wasn't evidence. It was a character assassination. They wanted to paint me as a zealot, a dangerous man spoiling for confrontation, rather than what I was: a father, a veteran, a citizen who had defended his own life when attacked by a violent extremist.

But while Ryan was busy playing politics in the courtroom, the world outside was proving my case for me.

On May 21st 2025, news broke out of Washington, D.C.: two Israeli embassy staffers were murdered by a man shouting, "Free Palestine." Headlines called it shocking. I didn't find it shocking at all. It was the same hatred I had seen on the streets of Boston, Quincy, and Newton—just taken to its logical, bloody conclusion.

Then on June 1st, another attack—this time in Colorado. A so-called activist targeted a peaceful vigil with Molotov cocktails and homemade flamethrowers, turning what should have been a moment of mourning into an inferno.

And suddenly, the question that Ryan's office kept circling back to—*why was I carrying a firearm that day?*—was no longer hypothetical. It wasn't paranoia. It wasn't posturing. It was reality. These weren't abstract threats. They were happening in real time, in American cities, to Jews and to anyone who dared stand with them.

My decision to carry wasn't just lawful—it was vindicated.

Then, the day after the attack in Boulder, just two weeks before trial, everything changed. After nearly a year of dragging me through the mud, of treating me like the criminal instead of the man who was attacked, Marian Ryan's office caved. They finally accepted my final offer. The charges would be dismissed. I would remain out of Newton until September 13, 2025—one year to the day after the attack. No probation. No jail. No guilty plea.

The timing was no accident. Ryan saw the writing on the wall. With terrorist attacks against Jews unfolding in Washington, Colorado, and elsewhere, she knew that prosecuting a man who had lawfully defended himself at a pro-Israel rally would look like exactly what it was: a political witch hunt. It would have been career suicide. So she backed down—not because it was right, not because she had the courage to admit error, but because self-preservation demanded it.

And then came the insult. Ryan and Newton's new police chief issued a joint statement, dripping with self-congratulation. They claimed that after "hundreds of hours of investigation," they had determined this was the "appropriate outcome."

Appropriate? No. Charges should have been dropped the very next day, once the 53-second 911 recording, the video evidence, and the eyewitness accounts were reviewed. Appropriate would have been acknowledging that I acted in self-defense. Appropriate would have been a public apology—for the shackles, the ankle monitor, the lost work, the humiliation. Instead, Ryan spun my survival into a narrative that protected her reputation while destroying mine.

That is the cost of politics in Massachusetts: truth is sacrificed, people are ground down, and justice is treated as a bargaining chip.

I spent nearly a year as a political prisoner in my own home—shunned by employers, ghosted by dates, smeared by headlines, and financially gutted. I had never gone without a job in my life, and suddenly my name was poison. I lost count of the applications I submitted, the interviews that seemed to go well until the background check. The polite rejection emails all read the same: *We've decided to go with another candidate.* Translation: *We Googled you.*

Dating was no different. Conversations that started warm and promising ended abruptly once they discovered my name in the news. My reputation had been weaponized against me. The scarlet letter of Ryan's prosecution clung to me everywhere I went.

And yet, despite it all, I would do it again.

Because on September 12, 2024, I stood for something bigger than myself. I stood for life. For Israel. For the Jewish people. For truth. I didn't act in hatred. I acted in love—love for my community, love for justice, love for survival.

That's the part Marian Ryan will never understand. She thought she could bend justice into a political weapon. But what I did that day wasn't politics. It was humanity.

So let me say this plainly, Marian Ryan: you failed. You failed me, you failed the people of Newton, and you failed the Jewish community you swore to protect. You turned an act of survival into a spectacle of politics. You weaponized your office not in the pursuit of justice, but in the preservation of your career.

You thought you could break me with shackles, curfews, and smears. You thought you could grind me down with court dates, headlines, and false narratives. You thought you could turn the truth into something negotiable. But here I stand. Still free. Still unbroken. Still willing to fight.

You may have stripped me of work, of money, of reputation, but you did not take my voice. You did not take my conviction. You did not take my purpose. On the day I was attacked, I acted to save lives. Every day since, I have acted to tell the truth. And no press release or political spin will ever erase that.

You wanted to make me an example. Fine—I'll be one. An example of how ordinary people must sometimes stand against both hatred in the streets and cowardice in the courthouse. An example of how justice belongs to the people, not to the politicians who manipulate it.

And when history looks back on this moment, Marian, it won't remember your press statements. It won't remember your excuses. It will remember that when evil struck Newton, I stood my ground—and you tried to punish me for it.

That is your legacy. Mine is still being written.

Chapter 19:
Still Standing — Faith Prevails

As I sit here dictating these words, one week shy of the one-year mark from the incident, I still struggle to put my thoughts into order. A year has passed, and yet in many ways the shockwaves are still moving through my life. I have faced war before — Bosnia, Kosovo, Iraq — and I have endured the kind of deployments that grind down body and soul. But I can say with certainty that this past year has been harder than any battlefield. If I were given the choice to spend two more years patrolling the dust and danger of Iraq or to relive this year, I would take Iraq without hesitation.

In twelve short months, I lost more than I thought possible. Friends drifted. The family turned distant. My reputation — built over decades of service, sacrifice, and loyalty — was smeared and questioned in ways that cut deep. Every decision I had ever made in my life, public or private, was suddenly up for judgment by people who barely knew me. I lost my job. I lost income. I lost stability. Piece by piece, the foundation of the life I had built was cracked and shaken.

And yet, in the same year that stripped me bare, I was also given something greater. I found family in places I never expected. Some who had once been casual companions revealed themselves to be brothers and sisters. They refused to let me falter. They sat with me through silence, brought meals to my doorstep, answered calls in the dead of night. They didn't let me collapse under the weight. They wouldn't allow me to surrender.

I know the life I had before September 12, 2024, is gone. That chapter is closed, and I am at peace with that truth. In its place, I've been given something new: clarity, purpose, and a mission.

This past year was not just hard — it was a crucible. The military had trained me to march for miles under load, to endure hunger and exhaustion, to fight when everything inside screamed for rest. But nothing could have prepared me for the isolation of house arrest, the humiliation of GPS shackles, the gut punch of being treated as a criminal for surviving. It is one thing to face an enemy in combat. In Iraq or Kosovo, the lines were clear. Here at home, the enemy wore no uniform. Sometimes it looked like a neighbor, a colleague, even a leader. They smiled politely in public but condemned me in whispers. They wielded power in headlines, not rifles. That was a different battlefield — one where betrayal cut deeper than bullets. And yet, I endured. Every false headline, every suspicious glance, every sleepless night under the weight of false accusations became proof that I could withstand more than I thought possible.

Conviction is cheap when it comes without consequence. But real conviction carries a cost. I discovered that my unwavering support for Israel and the Jewish people was, for some, unforgivable. Colleagues who once praised me grew silent or hostile. Institutions that claim to defend minorities had no interest in defending Jews. Politicians who should have stood beside me instead chose cowardice. In Iraq, conviction meant risking my life. In Massachusetts, conviction meant losing my livelihood, my reputation, and relationships I once thought unbreakable. Both demanded courage. Both came with scars.

But adversity strips away illusions. It reveals what's real. When the dust settled, I saw clearly who my people were. The ones who brought meals.

The ones who sat in silence. The ones who showed up at rallies, who packed the courtroom, who raised my bail on courthouse steps in minutes. They didn't need to promise me the world. Their presence was enough. It is said adversity reveals character. I say it reveals friendship. Those who stayed became family. And family is what sustained me when everything else was stripped away.

September 12, 2024, is my dividing line: before and after. That day will live with me forever. I do not regret my actions. My training, my instincts, my responsibility — all of it came to bear in those seconds. I acted to protect lives. I did what had to be done. And that is a truth no smear, no charge, no headline can erase.

But what happened that day wasn't only about me. It was a symptom of something larger: the resurgence of antisemitism in America. I have seen it up close — in schools, in union halls, in city meetings. The Massachusetts commission on antisemitism itself declared that antisemitism in K–12 schools is "pervasive and escalating." Yet silence reigns. If the same hate were aimed at any other minority, leaders would rush to condemn it. But because it is Jews, excuses are made, eyes are turned away, and lies are repackaged as justice. September 12 wasn't just about one man attacking me. It was about a culture that excuses hatred when Jews are the target.

The man I was before that day no longer exists. But I do not mourn him. Out of the ashes of that old life, something new has risen: a mission. I will not retreat into anonymity. My story is tied to that day, and I accept it. With it comes responsibility. My voice, my resolve — these are weapons in a larger fight. This is not only about my survival. It is about my daughter. About Jewish students sitting in classrooms where hate is ignored. About Jews walking city streets unsure of their safety. About Israel itself, the eternal homeland, under siege in every generation. My mission is simple: to stand in that space and say, "No further."

I don't know where this road leads. More battles lie ahead. More losses. More costs. But I know this: I will not bend. I will not break. I will not apologize for standing with Israel and the Jewish people. My resolve today is stronger than it was a year ago, stronger than the day I first put on a uniform, stronger than it was in Iraq or Kosovo. This is who I am. This is my life.

When the storm first broke, I thought it might break me. Instead, it remade me. This is my mission now: to stand in the way of Jewish hate, wherever it rises. To break the silence. To expose the lies. To fight for truth when others are too afraid. I don't know all that's coming. But I know how I'll face it: head up, shoulders back, never backing down.

They tried to shackle me. They tried to smear me. They tried to exile me. But they forgot one thing: I am not alone.

I stand with Israel. I stand with the Jewish people. I stand with the truth. And I will not back down. Not now. Not ever.

That is my promise. That is my life.

Epilogue

To whoever holds this book in their hands,

You've walked with me now—through Brookline and Bosnia, through Newton and Jerusalem, through courtrooms and candlelight vigils. You've seen what I've lost, and what I've found.

I never set out to write a story like this. I never imagined my life would be cracked open by violence on an American street, or that I'd spend a year fighting for the simple right to defend myself and stand with my friends. But here we are.

This past year has been the hardest of my life. Harder than Iraq. Harder than Kosovo. Harder than war. It tried to strip me bare—my work, my reputation, my peace. And yet, in the rubble, I found something more lasting: a mission, a family, a truth that cannot be shaken.

I have seen hate up close. I have felt its spit on my face, its fist around my throat, its lies printed in headlines. But I have also seen love. Friends showing up with food, strangers raising bail money, entire communities refusing to let me fall. That love is stronger than the hate. It has to be.

So if you take one thing from my story, let it be this: silence is not an option. Wherever you see hatred—against Jews, against Israel, against truth itself—you have a choice. You can look away, or you can stand. I chose to stand, and I will keep standing, no matter the cost.

As the Lubavitcher Rebbe once said: "Our very existence depends not on what we have already achieved, but on our constant determination to persevere, to go forward, and never to give up."

That is my promise. That is my life. I will never give up. And I will never be silent.

Acknowledgements

No journey is ever walked alone. This book, and the life it reflects, could never have been written without the love, strength, and faith of those who stood beside me.

To **Sarah O.**, for your friendship, encouragement, and unwavering support when the road grew dark — thank you for reminding me that light is never too far away.

To **Chabad**, for opening your doors and your hearts, showing me that faith is not only tradition, but family and belonging.

To my **veteran brothers**, who carried me through fire, across oceans, and into battles both seen and unseen. ROTL

To the **Jewish community**, for welcoming me as one of your own, standing shoulder to shoulder against hate, and teaching me what it means to endure with dignity.

To my **Iranian brother and sister** who reminded me that courage and truth can come from unexpected places, and that even across borders and histories, people of conscience stand together.

To **Hashem**, who tests but never abandons, whose presence guided me through fire and shadow, and whose hand steadied me when my own faith faltered.

And above all, to **my mom and my daughter**. Mom, your love has given me hope and your support my constant strength. To Jimmy, you are my heart, my reason, and my future — every page of this book is for you.

About the author

Scott Hayes is a U.S. Army veteran who served in Bosnia, Kosovo, and Iraq. Raised in Brookline, Massachusetts, in an Irish-Catholic family, he forged an enduring connection with the Jewish community, one that would shape his convictions and his life's mission.

In September 2024, while standing at a pro-Israel rally in Newton, Massachusetts, Scott's life was forever changed when a terrorist attack forced him to act in self-defense. The aftermath plunged him into a public legal battle that tested his character, his resilience, and his faith. What was meant to silence him instead solidified his resolve.

Scott is an active leader in the activist community against antisemitism, he has dedicated himself to strengthening Jewish pride and support for Israel. He works closely with educators, advocates, and community members to confront antisemitism in all its forms and ensure that Jewish voices are heard and respected. Through his efforts, he has played a pivotal role in uniting people across Massachusetts and beyond, building bridges of understanding, and empowering others to stand proudly and unapologetically against hate. Today, Scott continues to speak out against antisemitism and champion the cause of Israel. He lives in Massachusetts, where he raises his daughter, serves his community, and carries forward his mission with the same resolve that guided him through the battlefield and the courtroom alike

www.ingramcontent.com/pod-product-compliance
Lightning Source LLC
Chambersburg PA
CBHW070618030426
42337CB00020B/3847